Teaching Reading and Spelling to Dyslexic Children

Getting to Grips with Words

Margaret Walton

David Fulton Publishers
London

David Fulton Publishers Ltd
Ormond House, 26–27 Boswell Street, London WC1N 3JZ

www.fultonpublishers.co.uk

First published in Great Britain by David Fulton Publishers 1998
Reprinted 1998, 2000 (twice)

Note: The right of Margaret Walton to be identified as the author of this work has been asserted by her in accordance with the Copyright, Designs and Patents Act 1988.

British Library Cataloguing in Publication Data
A catalogue record for this book is available from the British Library

ISBN 1–85346–565–8

Typeset by Textype Typesetters, Cambridge
Printed in Great Britain by Bell & Bain Ltd, Glasgow

Contents

Chart 2

Punctuation

Spelling

Books

Appendices

Foreword

Professor T. R. Miles

There is now a consensus that, as far as the English language is concerned, dyslexic children can be taught to read and spell most words if they receive systematic instruction in the sounds made by individual letters and combinations of letters. In this connection I cannot do better than quote the wise words of the great American pioneer, Margaret Rawson: what is needed, in her view, is 'a program that is at once: *structured, sequential, cumulative,* and *thorough* . . . The skills are to be learned through all the avenues of learning open to the student – *visual, auditory,* and *tactile-kinesthetic in interaction* (our familiar multisensory approach) (Rawson, 1970, p. 118).

There is now no shortage of books and materials which embody such teaching methods. What particularly impresses me about Margaret Walton's book is its *freshness*. She somehow breathes life into material which in the wrong hands might seem tedious and arid. I do not see how any parent or teacher, reading this book, can fail to be inspired by Margaret's enthusiasm. Dyslexics have certain physiologically-caused limitations which are beyond their control, and it is for this reason that spelling (in particular) does not come easily to them. However, if learning to spell can be presented to the pupil as a challenge, and if success, even on a modest scale, is liberally praised, the task need not be unbearably stressful.

Margaret is not one to minimise difficulties. For example, some spellings are what she calls 'unexpected' – 'their', 'your', 'said', etc., and the spelling of these words cannot be built up by putting together their individual sounds; many dyslexics are liable to confuse 'b' and 'd', and as they grow older they have difficulty with other literacy matters such as acquiring a knowledge of punctuation. She recognises, too, that a classroom spelling test may be a traumatic experience for some dyslexic children (and there is in fact research evidence that such stresses can be long lasting; see Everatt and Brennan, 1996).

As is made clear in the introduction, this is a book for parents and for non-specialist teachers. I was told, over 40 years ago, that parents should not try to teach their own children because they were 'too emotionally involved'. I have never subscribed to this view. Even if there is the occasional 'scrap' (which there need not be) it is a small price to pay for the child's achievement of literacy.

I warmly commend this book and hope it will be widely read.

Professor T. R. Miles, M.A., Ph.D., C.Psychol., FBPsS

References

Everatt, J. and Brannan, P. (1996) The effects of a spelling task on the subsequent performance of dyslexics. *Dyslexia*, 2, 1, 22–30.

Rawson, M.B. (1970) The structure of English: the language to be learned. *Bulletin of the Orton Society*, 20, 103–23.

Acknowledgements

I have learnt a lot from the children I have taught, and I am grateful to them. They have been unwitting 'guinea pigs' for many of my ideas. Added to which, Huw and James have kindly allowed me to reproduce their pictures.

My colleagues, Janet Chapman, Dorothy Gilroy, Liz Du Pré and Eileen Stirling have been generous with their help and encouragement. I owe an even bigger debt to my friend Joy Cave, and to Ann Cooke, Director of the Dyslexia Unit, University of North Wales, Bangor.

Lastly, thanks to my husband Ken, who has 'lived' with this book for many years.

'Chaotic', 'unpredictable', 'disorganised', 'a mess' – these are just a few of the more repeatable expressions used to describe English spelling.

David Crystal
The English Language

Introduction

Who is this book for?

This book was written for two groups of people.

Firstly, it was written for parents who want to help their child who is finding reading and spelling difficult. Parents often say, 'I want to help but I don't know how!' It was this remark that encouraged me to write this book. Sometimes a parent takes on the role of teacher because specialist help is not available. If this is the case, this parent has a hard task ahead of her but this book will help. By contrast, another child may be having special lessons in reading and spelling, and the parent just wants to understand what is going on as her child learns to read and spell.

The other group who can be helped by this book are non-specialist teachers who have no experience in teaching reading and spelling to pupils who have difficulty with these skills. Many talented, qualified teachers fall into this group and some of them are keen to help a particular pupil who is obviously intelligent, but whose written work is almost unintelligible. Although these teachers may only be able to devote the odd minute or two to an individual pupil, that minute will be more valuable if the teacher has some knowledge of the common letter combinations and the sounds they represent.

So, parents and non-specialist teachers, this book was written for you!

Notes – gender, age, tolerance and photocopying

Gender

Did you notice that I referred to a parent as 'she'? To simplify things I refer to parents and teachers as 'she', and pupils as 'he'.

Age

You will notice too, that I often seem to be talking about teaching a young child. I have taught all ages, from six to sixty, and they all need to learn the same things in order to read and spell, but of course the approach you use will vary, and the books or magazines that a child will enjoy will be very different from those that will appeal to a teenager or adult.

Tolerance

Critical readers may come across some statements in this book that are not strictly accurate. I hope that these people will be understanding. Sometimes, in order to give a simple explanation that covers the vast majority of cases, it is necessary to be less than 100 per cent accurate.

Photocopying

I have put all the photocopiable material at the back of this book. You can see it on pages 106–26.

Sections in this book

The main part of this book is in three sections. The first section gives general information about teaching reading and spelling.

The second section concerns Chart 1 which can be seen on page 106. It covers the earlier stages in learning to read and spell. There is nothing particularly original about this chart. I have simply arranged the sounds neatly. Some children learn these sounds without too much trouble and their reading problems become obvious only when they are faced with more difficult work. However, I would advise you not to skip Chart 1, even if it is only to check that the pupil really does know everything on it. Usually there are some gaps in his knowledge and it is as well to fill these gaps before continuing. When the chart is used simply as a useful check, it can be worked through very quickly, perhaps in a couple of sessions. On the other hand, young children, or pupils with severe difficulties, may need several weeks or even months to complete this work.

The third section is about Chart 2 which can be seen on page 116. I designed this chart while teaching the later stages in learning to read and spell. There is a huge amount of work summarised on this chart. It will take a long time to learn all the sounds represented here. Some pupils take two years, others even longer. However, even when the work is only partly completed, the chart is a very useful memory aid.

In other smaller sections I deal with basic punctuation, confusion over *two*, *to* and *too*, as well as *there* and *their*. I also discuss dictionaries and electronic spellcheckers, and give book lists. In the final section you will find all the photocopiable material you need to use this book effectively.

General Information

When we read and write we are using a code

Think of the four ways we use language – speaking and listening, reading and writing. Imagine how these forms of language developed among the first humans. At a very early stage they probably made sounds to communicate with each other, and gradually these sounds evolved into some kind of spoken language. The skill of listening to and understanding speech must have developed alongside early spoken language. Eventually people made marks, little pictures or signs to represent the sounds of their speech and these developed into writing. Writing, therefore, can be thought of as a code that represents the sounds of speech. When people learn the *code* they can *decode* the marks and translate them back into the sounds of speech, in other words they can read. Learning to use the code is what learning to read and write is all about.

Take a different example that we all know about. Babies listen and imitate sounds and these sounds gradually develop into understandable speech. Then, several years later, they learn to use the code that represents speech sounds on paper, in other words they learn to write. At the same time they learn to decode writing, or to put it into everyday words, they learn to read. Generally children learn to listen and speak fairly easily, but learning the code for reading and spelling is not so easy. The aim of this book is to help people to understand more about our English reading and spelling code and consequently improve their reading and spelling.

Considering the examples above, it is reasonable to use a method of teaching reading and spelling based on the sounds of our speech. This is the Phonic Method.

The Phonic Method

Some people are uncertain about the word 'phonic'; they needn't be. Just think of the word 'phone'. A phone is an instrument for carrying *sound*. 'Phonic' and 'phone' are just two versions of the same word, and the Phonic Method of teaching is based on the *sounds* of the letters, which are different from their names. The difference between the *sounds* and the names of letters is explained on page 14.

Most children learn to read and write by whatever method a school uses, but I firmly believe that those who have difficulty with reading and spelling learn best when the Phonic Method of teaching is used. If a child learns to read by this method, he can tackle an enormous number of words he has never seen before.

My two charts are based on the Phonic Method and they help pupils to spell words according to phonic rules. They help with reading too, enabling a child to build words by running together the sounds of the individual letters or letter combinations.

However, the Phonic Method does not hold the key to all English words. It helps with *Regular words*, that is words which obey the phonic rules. A BBC Literacy Pack stated that 85 per cent of our words use regular, recurring phonic patterns. 'That's all very well', you say, 'but what about the other 15 per cent? That's a sizable chunk not accounted for! How are we supposed to tackle those words?' The answer is that a second, supplementary teaching method is needed for teaching *Irregular words*, those that you might call the awkward words, that don't obey the phonic rules.

The 'Look and Say' Method, and using flash cards

'Look and Say' is the secondary method that I use for teaching awkward, *Irregular words*. Here are a few examples of regular and irregular words.

PHONIC (Regular)	LOOK AND SAY (Irregular)
red	said
horse	people
interesting	come

It is impossible to build **said, people** and **come** from the sounds of the letters. For example, if you tried to do so, **come** would sound the same as **comb**. If you are puzzled by this, think of **home**, which is a regular word. If **come** was regular, it would rhyme with **home**. All the regular words listed above can be built using phonic rules. I will be explaining more about building words later. You need to know the sounds on Chart 2 to build **horse** and **interesting**.

Irregular words are presented as whole words and simply have to be learnt. The pupil has to 'Look and Say' them. Flash cards are extremely useful for learning these words. Each card has a single word written on it. Teachers use large flash cards in the classroom but flash cards for home can be made much smaller. I use strips of thin card about an inch wide, cut from cereal packets. These are convenient for shuffling about on a table or fixing to the fridge door with little magnets.

Use flash cards often, but only for short sessions. I use them like this. To begin, I hold all the cards. I put them onto the table one at a time, on top of each other as fast as I think is reasonable for that particular pupil to read them. If he cannot say the correct word I put that card on my side of the table. All the ones he reads correctly, he 'wins'. You could keep a record of the number he wins each time as an incentive to improve his score. The ones he fails to read can go up on the fridge door until the next game. I think between 10 and 20 cards is a reasonable number to use to keep the game light-hearted. As the pupil gets very good at reading the words in the pack, I negotiate with him about removing some cards so that he can have one or two new words put in. The cards which are taken out of the pack are kept, and once in a while we have a mammoth game with all the cards and see what his grand total is.

Don't be tempted to use flash cards for regular words, otherwise you'll end up with masses and masses of them.

These are some of the most useful early 'Look and Say' words. Introduce them gradually as the pupil needs them.

he	the	are	said	we	I
be	so	you	of	was	one
she	come	there	two	to	they

The bad news is that many of the words we use most often are irregular; the good news is that the very fact that we use them so much, often helps the children to learn them.

I read recently that the word *the* accounts for about 11 per cent of written English. If this is true, it means that a pupil who can write *the* will get 11 per cent of the words he writes correct. That's quite an encouraging thought!

The 'Real Books' Method

A word about the 'Real Books' Method of teaching reading. This method recommends that children have access to 'real books', as opposed to books in a reading scheme with carefully controlled vocabulary and short sentences. I feel that children should have access to all kinds of books, but people who have great difficulty in reading will not get much from books with difficult words and long, involved sentences, unless those books have clear pictures or diagrams which, of course, can convey information without relying on reading skills.

Regional pronunciation

English pronunciation varies in different parts of Britain and indeed throughout the world. Be especially considerate if your pupil uses different pronunciation from you. This problem often occurs with words like *bath*. In some parts of Britain people pronounce this with an *ar* sound (as in *star*), but I grew up using a short ă as in *apple*. (See next section.) I find that one way of helping children who write *barth* (a logical spelling of what they say) is to get them to imitate me, which they usually think is very funny, and then 'listen to my voice inside their head' when they want to spell the word.

Short and long vowels

As you will see in the examples below, using long vowels is not as straightforward as using short ones. Chart 2 deals with long vowel letter combinations and I explain more about them on page 34.

Short vowels		Long vowels	
ă	apple, cat	ā	acorn, gate, paid
ĕ	egg, pen	ē	equal, theme, dream
ĭ	ink, bin	ī	idea, tide, fly
ŏ	orange, pot	ō	open, rope, crow
ŭ	umbrella, run	ū	uniform, tube, new

Mispronunciation

Quite a different problem arises when a child mispronounces a word because he has never learnt to say it properly. Confusion between *free* and *three* is a good example of this. Tact, sympathy and practice are the only suggestions I can make to overcome this difficulty. Some pupils enjoy putting their tongue out at the teacher whenever they have to pronounce *th*. Others would rather put their tongue out at their reflection in a small mirror. If it is the very first time they have ever pronounced *th* properly, they will probably feel quite strange!

Two types of spelling mistakes

I divide spelling mistakes into two types:

1. 'a bad mistake' when phonic reading of the word does not produce the right sound, e.g. *brid* for *bird*, *slep* for *sleep*.
2. 'a good try' when phonic reading produces a recognisable word, e.g. *elifunt* for *elephant*, *sleav* for *sleeve*.

Teaching hints

Teachers may want to skip this section but I have included it because I think it will be useful to many parents.

Use a multisensory approach

We all learn by using our senses, and it is best to teach in a way that uses as many of them as possible. Attack a problem from as many sides as possible, because learning through one sense reinforces learning through another. Think of how a pupil uses his *eyes* to see letters and words; his *ears* to listen to their sounds; his *mouth, tongue and teeth* to say them; and his *fingers* to write them. Sometimes he can use his larger muscles too. For example, a young pupil may enjoy writing letters in sand, or trying to make the shape of a letter with his whole body. Sounding out the letters or, later on, the syllables, as he writes words is a very old-fashioned technique, but still very useful.

Motivation

Some children who have difficulty with reading and spelling want to learn these skills; other children do not seem to care about them. Sometimes a pupil has struggled with reading and spelling for several years and has had extremely poor results. No wonder he has lost interest. This lack of motivation is difficult to overcome. Think for a moment, why do we read? It's usually to get information, such as following a recipe or finding out what's on television, but sometimes it's for pure pleasure and entertainment. The best way of encouraging a child to read is to read aloud to him so that he associates reading with pleasure. You must, of course, be prepared to read what he wants to hear! There will be other occasions when he needs some information, perhaps instructions about building a model or how to send away for a free offer on the cornflakes box. By reading to him on these occasions you are showing him how useful it is being able to read. For a long time he will want stories and information from books that are far too difficult for him to tackle on his own. If the struggle is too great he will simply give up, discouraged, and valuable ground will be lost. By reading the more difficult books aloud to him, you will also be increasing his vocabulary, which is very important. If you discuss what you have been reading, you can check that he has understood it, and he will gradually start to use some of the new words.

Show that writing is useful too, not just for school work, but in everyday life. Short notes, like 'Gon to Freds back harf pats 8', are very useful, even if the spelling is not perfect. If you can decode the note, then the main object of giving a message has been achieved. Jotting down phone messages, sending birthday or Christmas cards and making shopping lists are all occasions when most of us write, without giving it a second thought. Try to involve the pupil in these short but useful bits of writing, which are so different from writing an essay in school. It is better to write something that is incorrect but readable, than to feel that it is useless or too embarrassing to try.

Many children who struggle with spelling, have difficulty in completing a piece of written work, but it is important that they do finish it. If they get into the habit of not finishing work, they will start to feel that they might as well not bother to start anything in the first place. On the other hand, a finished piece of work is an achievement, something to be proud of, especially if it has cost them considerable effort. If a pupil gets stuck with his work, try to find out what is holding him up. Sometimes a solution occurs to a pupil even as he tries to put his problems into words. Often a pupil feels that the task is just too big for him to cope with. If this is the case, discuss how it can be broken up into a series of smaller tasks, and then tackle one bit at a time.

Reading

It may strike you as strange but one of the best ways of helping a young child to start reading is to read to him. It's a good idea for him to choose the book, but you may have to guide him towards something simple with few words and interesting pictures that you can talk about. It doesn't matter if he wants the same book over and over again. Gradually involve him in the reading, perhaps by seeing if he can recognise the name of the child in the story, or even the first letter of the name. He will be able to read a complete little story for himself quite soon if the words in the story are mainly phonic.

The 'Primary Phonics' series are excellent for this stage. Always listen to him read, and support and encourage him when necessary. It's better that he should read fluently through several stories that are well within his capabilities, and enjoy the sweet sensation of success, than that he should struggle with a book that is just that bit too difficult for him.

A very relaxed way of helping and encouraging a young child with his reading is called 'Shared Reading'. This is something that many parents do already, very naturally. Imagine a child enjoying a book curled up with Mum or Dad. Fun, cuddles and pleasure are a natural outcome of this situation which has now been given the label 'Shared Reading'. Most of the reading will be done by the adult but interruptions and little discussions are all part of the learning process. The most important aspect of 'Shared Reading' is that it connects books and reading with pleasure.

Another way to help and support a child, who is reading a book that has some words that will bring him to a halt, is to use 'Paired Reading'. This technique is particularly suitable for parents helping their children. The parent and the child read the words together. The parent has to slow her speed slightly to suit the child. When a difficult word crops up, the parent will automatically pronounce it a fraction ahead of the child. His eyes will travel over the word as he repeats it only a split second after his Mum. 'Paired Reading' keeps the momentum going, encourages fluency and boosts the child's morale. There should be no stress because these sessions are not for building words. You are reading for enjoyment and meaning. Take time to discuss the story and the pictures.

There is no reason why you shouldn't switch between these methods during one reading session. Whichever of these techniques you use, be conscious of how much effort your pupil is making. Give him lots of praise when he succeeds; and help, encouragement and sympathy when he does not. Keep reading sessions pleasant and try to end on a happy and successful note.

Sometimes an older pupil is keen to read a book which is too difficult for him, and 14–16 year olds have to read novels like 'A Kestrel for a Knave' by Barry Hines, as part of their English course. They despair at the thought of getting through a book of 160 or so pages, and yet they need to know the book thoroughly in order to cope with their National Curriculum course work.

I taught a teenager who found out which book they were going to study in the Autumn Term and borrowed a copy to read during the Summer holidays. He religiously read a set number of pages each week. 'Wonderful!', you may think, but when I asked a few simple questions about events in the story, he hadn't the faintest idea of the answers. The effort involved in reading had been so great that he hadn't been able to take in the meaning of the words. It was heartbreaking.

The very best solution to this problem is for someone else to read the book onto tape. This takes a lot of time and many parents are too busy, but perhaps a grandparent or friend who has retired may be willing to do it. It is quite cheap and easy to send audio tapes through the post, using a paddy bag and a second class stamp, so it doesn't matter if the reader lives at the other end of the country. The recordings can be made a chapter at a time, when it suits the reader, and of course the child can listen to the tapes at times that suit him, perhaps in bed just before he goes to sleep, or when he's having a bath or shower, or during a car journey. Some children like to listen to a tape and follow the text at the same time. If this is the case, the reader should include some signal, like two claps, when she turns over a page. This will help the child to find his place again if he loses it.

Many adults throw up their hands in horror at the thought of reading aloud to a recording machine. I sympathise with them. It's a bit unnerving. Read through a chapter first, so that you know the story, and then shut yourself away from the rest of the family and have a go. You will probably find that it's not as bad as you think. It doesn't have to be perfect. The pupil will be so pleased that someone is helping him with the enormous effort of getting through the book, that he will not mind a few mistakes and stumbles. The reader may even find that she is enjoying the story.

If the reader is a parent, it may be easier to read the book aloud to the child. This will also give you both the chance to discuss anything that the child doesn't quite understand. Reading a set book for a pupil is not 'cheating'. His English work is not meant to test his reading ability.

The number of books available on audio tapes is growing rapidly and you may be able to buy, or borrow from your local library, the one your child is studying. This sounds like the ideal option. The reading will be excellent and your child will be practising his listening skills, which is important too. However, you may find that it is impossible to follow the text while listening to the tape, because many tapes are abridged. If this is the case, I would put the book aside and enjoy the tape. You can always come back to the book later.

Many children have to study a play by Shakespeare and this is not easy, even for fluent readers. Several of his plays have been made into half-hour animated films and are available on video-tapes. These are excellent for arousing the children's interest and covering the essential elements of the story. Full length performances are also available. Check with your local library or video shop and see if the play you want is available.

If a book is only slightly too difficult, you and the pupil can tackle it together in several different ways. One way is to read alternate paragraphs for him. This helps the flow of the story and he will still do quite a lot of reading.

However, if you feel he needs more help, in order to get some fun and satisfaction from that particular book, you can read nearly every word. Speak at a slightly slower pace than normal and point to the words as you go along. Every now and then stop for him to read the next word. He has to follow closely because he doesn't know when you are going to stop. This technique usually goes down very well. Waiting for the stops makes it rather like Musical Chairs. The improved pace of the story helps the pupil to get the meaning from the words and gives him a model for fluency and intonation.

Spelling

Reading brings its own rewards but this is not usually the case with spelling. Many pupils don't get much satisfaction from a list of correctly spelt words. After all, we usually write things correctly for the benefit or approval of someone else. It doesn't really matter if we make mistakes on a shopping list which no-one else is going to see. Consequently, progress in spelling usually lags behind progress in reading, but it is important to work at both skills together because they help each other.

Spelling tests are often regarded as a kind of torture by people who are not good at spelling. Even good spellers are often either anxious about them, or find them deadly boring. However, they become more interesting if you break them up by checking, every now and then, that the pupil knows the meanings of the words. This gives him practice in finding the right words when he is speaking, which will help him when he has to do the same in written words. Encourage the pupil to ask if he is uncertain about the meaning of a word. People sometimes pick up meanings that are not quite right; sometimes they are completely wrong. When you define a word, use it in one or two sentences, and then ask the child to make up a sentence using it.

A short spelling test in a one-to-one situation should be quite different from a spelling test in a classroom. Don't give the whole test before you correct it and award a mark, if indeed you want to give a mark. Instead, stop the pupil if he is spelling a word wrongly and ask him to build and read what he has written. If he is unsure, you read it. Perhaps he has written *sti* when he was trying to write *string*. When he hears *sti* he will often realise his mistake and correct it himself. This encourages the habit of checking his own spelling. If he can't put his mistake right, help him with the part of the word that is causing trouble. Don't help him with the whole word if he can manage some of it himself. By giving a spelling test in this way you are 'on his side', supporting him and revising previous work. The test becomes another teaching method, a positive, creative and cooperative activity. As for the final mark, this is a matter of negotiation between teacher and pupil. You may be surprised at how scrupulously fair the pupil will be, refusing to take a full mark for a word which has been a joint effort. Do you remember about my two kinds of spelling mistake which I explained on page 6? I take off one mark for 'a bad mistake', but only half a mark for 'a good try'.

You may find the 'Look, Say, Cover, Write, Check' routine helpful when practising spelling. Write the selected words in a column on the left of the page. The pupil then covers them with a strip of paper. Then he looks carefully at the first word, says it, covers it, writes it on the same line, and then uncovers it again and checks it for himself.

When a pupil is checking his spelling after writing a passage, he may find it useful to start at the end and work backwards. This makes him look at each word separately and will stop him reading what he *thinks* he has written, rather than what he *has* written.

Using audio tapes for spelling tests

All my pupils, whatever their age, like using audio tapes to give themselves spelling tests. First the pupil selects a list of words. The words may all contain a particular letter combination that he is learning, or they may be awkward 'Look and Say' words, or a mixture of these. Then he reads out these words and records them onto a tape, leaving quite long pauses between the words. When the tape is played, he will find that he needs a good pause after each word to give him time to switch off the recorder and write down the word. When he has written that word the machine is switched on briefly to give the next word, and so he continues to the end. You may say that a pupil will choose words that are too easy, but a teacher can see which words have been used by glancing at the child's exercise book. If a teacher wants a child to practise certain words, then she can record those words onto the tape, or at least make a list of them.

Pupils need a lot of practice and revision to help them remember letter combinations. Use as many different ways of practising these as you can – completing sentences with missing words, games, dictation, puzzles, simple crosswords and inventing silly phrases, as well as spelling tests. Whenever possible use words that are linked to the pupil's particular interests to make these exercises more useful and enjoyable.

Cloze exercises

In a cloze exercise the pupil is given a passage that has several words missing. He has to fill in the gaps with sensible words. When he does this he is practising several skills.

- Reading
- Comprehension (thinking, and understanding the passage)
- Vocabulary (being able to produce a suitable word)
- Spelling

Here is a simple cloze passage.

I .... a dog and his name .... Rex. He is black and .... He likes to .... for walks on .... beach. Sometimes he .... in the sea. When he comes .... he shakes himself and drops of .... fly in all directions.

Sometimes there is more than one suitable word. For example, the dog could be black and *white*, or black and *brown*, or even black and *large* or *small*. Any of these would be acceptable. Tell your pupil to read through the whole passage first, saying the word 'something' every time he comes to a blank. He will then have a pretty good idea of the words he needs to put in.

If your pupils find this type of exercise difficult you could supply suitable words. In this case I would give,

     is   swims   out   the   have   go   white   water

Another option is to write the first letter of each missing word in the blank spaces.

You can make up your own cloze passages by taking a piece from one of his books. On the other hand, you might find it easier to start with a picture cut from a magazine, catalogue or food packet. Get your pupil to talk about the picture and quickly scribble down what he says. Then re-write it, missing out every seventh or eighth word. He will then be practising reading and writing his own words, which are the words he is most likely to need in his own free writing.

Conclusion

'Comparisons are odious!' There is nothing to be gained by comparing a pupil's work with that of his friends or members of his family. The only useful comparison is with his own previous performance and that should only be done occasionally, especially when a decided improvement will be seen. Always adopt a positive attitude and never miss an opportunity to praise and encourage.

One of the most important skills a teacher uses is the ability to judge the difficulty of a piece of work so that the pupil has to make some effort, but will almost certainly succeed. This is only possible by watching the pupil's performance carefully. When a pupil who is trying fails, the teacher has failed. But even good teachers do not win every time! Don't be discouraged. If you fail to explain a point, think of the 'failure' as a learning process that will improve your teaching technique. It is simply a sign that another approach is needed. The child who finds difficulty with reading and spelling is probably never going to be first class in either, particularly spelling, but it is important for him to do them well enough to deal with everyday life. If this is to happen, both teacher and pupil will have to spend a lot of time and effort. The teacher must always be the pupil's helper and lessons must never become a battle. They should be short and frequent and, most importantly, pleasant and successful. Be proud of small victories. When they occur, you have both earned the right to be pleased with yourselves.

Organising the pupil's work

One sign of dyslexia is poor organisational skills, so encouraging your pupil to be organised is valuable training for him. Find suitable boxes for his alphabet picture cards, letter cards, 'Look and Say' flash cards etc., and have a special place for these boxes and his reading and spelling books.

Many pupils suffer from having spelling rules and word lists that they are trying to learn mixed up with exercises that are peppered with mistakes and crossings-out. This is very confusing. It is much better to have two completely different books for the pupil's work.

The pupil should have a *hard-backed A4 book* (about 20 × 30 cm). Usually I am the only person who writes in this book because it must have no mistakes. However, if a pupil has very neat handwriting, he writes in it and I check his lists carefully to make sure that the spellings are correct. This hard-backed book becomes a personal reference book: 'personal', because the pupil is involved in choosing what goes into it; 'reference', because the pupil refers to it constantly. Several pages at the front are used for a list of Contents. All the pages are numbered as they are used; the two charts are stuck inside the front and back covers, where they will always be readily available and easily found. The main part of the book contains word lists to illustrate each sound that is taught. Each page has only one sound on it, even if there are very few words which have that particular sound. This book becomes a valuable reference source that the pupil uses confidently because he has seen it being made and knows his way around it. Knowing how this book is organised will give him confidence when using other reference books, and this is a very useful additional skill.

All his other work, such as exercises, crosswords, spelling tests, dictations, pictures, stories etc. should be done in an ordinary exercise book.

When I feel it is appropriate, I provide a small indexed notebook, (about 10 × 16 cm) for awkward, irregular words that my pupil constantly spells incorrectly. These are words that we can't include in the word lists in the hard-backed book because, of course, the words in there are regular. Words like *said* and *does* are likely to give trouble. The fact that the book is indexed, and has only a few words in it, means that the child can open it at the right page immediately and find the word quickly.

Later on, when more irregular words are being used, your pupil may like to have a copy of Eileen Stirling's *Spelling Check-list* which lists about 700 words that dyslexics find particularly troublesome.

Chart 1

Introduction

Please look at the complete Chart 1 on page 106. It represents the earliest steps in learning to read and spell. You will see that it is in three sections. The first section shows the alphabet in capital letters and in small letters (sometimes called upper and lower case) arranged in the shape of a rainbow. The middle section is called Unexpected Sounds and the third section is called Blends. As I said in my Introduction, Chart 1 may only be needed as a rapid check or revision and can be worked through quickly. Even if this is so, stick a copy of this Chart inside the front cover of the hard-backed book for future reference. It's surprising how pupils who are quite advanced in their spelling write *banck* or *kwick* and need to look at Chart 1 to see that we don't use *-nck* or *kw-*.

I have included a smaller version of Chart 1 that will fit into an exercise book. It is on page 123.

If your pupil is just starting to learn the sounds of the alphabet, and will take some time to cope with the whole of the Chart, you could photocopy the full size Chart, cut it into three sections and stick one section at a time in his exercise book. When he knows all the sounds, you can then stick a complete photocopy into the front of his hard-backed book.

Section 1 The alphabet

Look at the top section of the chart and, for the moment, ignore the lower two sections. Arranging the letters in a rainbow shape helps the pupil to learn the order of the letters, which he will need to know when he starts to use a dictionary. Point out that *m* and *n* are in the middle of the alphabet.

Consonants and vowels

You will see that, in both alphabets, the letters *a e i o u* have been boxed. Just to stress them even more, I have repeated them underneath the 'rainbow'. Highlight them in red. These are very special letters; they are *vowels*. All the other letters are *consonants*. Every word, no matter how small, has to have at least one vowel. Even the words *'a'* and *'I'* have a vowel, don't they? Some words have lots of vowels. At this stage I don't class *y* as a vowel because in the early stages of reading it is used only as a consonant. When the pupil is learning the sounds on Chart 2, *y* is introduced as a vowel and will be written in the empty box under the 'rainbow' and above the *i*.

Chart 1   13

Capital letters and small letters (upper case and lower case)

Children should be familiar with small letters and capitals. It is important not to use both kinds together unless there is a good reason for doing so. We use small letters most. Capital letters are used to begin sentences, and to start names of people, rivers, mountains and places etc., for example, David, Mrs. Johnson, the Nile, Snowdon, Manchester and Africa. Capital letters are all the same size. They have no tails hanging down or tall backs standing up. That is why we use them for filling in forms and doing crosswords.

The sounds of the letters are different from their names

Many people do not understand that the *sounds* of letters are not the same as their *names*. For example, the sound of the first letter of *fat* is like air escaping from a puncture, whereas its name is pronounced *eff*. Similarly, the first letter of *house* sounds like a sigh, but its name is pronounced *aitch*. The sound of *x* often defeats parents, especially as there are no common words starting with this letter. The solution is to use a word like *box* and then isolate the last sound of the word. You will find that it is produced near the back of the mouth and sounds like *ks*.

Adults often find it difficult to switch over to using the sounds instead of the names of letters. Of course, eventually, children need to know both but, in the early stages, the names of letters do not help with reading and spelling. Let me show you what I mean. If you say that *cat* is spelt *see ay tea* it is impossible to run *see-ay-tea* together and hear anything that sounds like *cat*. If a non-reader hears *bee yellow tea*, what is he to make of it? The answer is on page 103 if you can't work it out.

There are many beautifully illustrated ABC books in the bookshops, but some of them use inappropriate pictures if you are trying to teach a child the sounds of the letters. For example, *giraffe* is no good for the letter *g*, but *gorilla* is fine. The sound of the letter *g* in *giraffe* is like the *j* in *jam*, whereas the sound of the *g* in *gorilla* is like the *g* in *garden*. I recently saw a book that included *a* for *acorn*, *c* for *chair* and *u* for *unicorn*. It should have had something like *a* for *arrow*, *c* for *cow*, and *u* for *umbrella*, *umpire* or *upstairs*.

If you are confused by this, say the words slowly and listen carefully to the very first sound that you make for each word.

Alphabet pictures and letter cards

If your pupil is young, you can make two sets of small cards, one showing the letters of the alphabet, and the other with pictures to match the letters. I have provided you with letters and pictures on pages 108–10. You can either photocopy these pages onto thin card and cut them up, or make your own, if you prefer to. If you choose to draw your own pictures, check that the first letter of the word makes the correct sound. Remember about the giraffe and the gorilla in the previous section. My picture cards are square (5cm × 5cm) and the pictures that represent vowels have a border that you should colour red.

You will see that my letter cards, on pages 110–11, are rectangular (5cm × 2.5cm). This is so that the letters are not too far apart when the cards are used to build words. Notice that my letters sit on a line. When a child starts to use lined paper for writing, encourage him to sit his letters on a line in the same way. Using a line also helps to sort out the *p*s and *b*s. Colour the letter cards that represent the vowels red, or put a red border round them, so that they match the picture cards for the vowels. This reinforces the idea that these are special letters. Your letter cards should look like this.

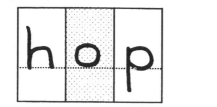 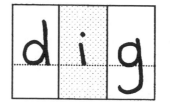

Each time you teach a sound, introduce a picture card and a matching letter card. The cards can be used to practise matching pictures and letters. Vary this matching game, sometimes start with the pictures, sometimes with the letters, and sometimes with a mixture of both. When a pupil gets very good at this, I tell him that I am going to match the pictures and letters, making some mistakes. He has to see if he can find the mistakes and put them right.

There are some attractive sets of letters and pictures in the shops. If you are about to buy some, check that the names of the pictured objects really do start with the correct sound. Also watch out for capital letters. They are fine if you are teaching capital letters, but can be very confusing if they are mixed up with lower case letters too soon.

Don't try to teach all twenty six letters straight away. It's surprising how many words you can make with just a few letters. For example, if you teach the vowels *a* and *i*, and the consonants *t*, *m*, *n*, *p*, *h* and *s*, you will find that you can build at least twenty five words. Here's a selection.

a

tan	tap	mat	man	map	Sam
pat	pan	hat	ham	has	sat

i

tin	Tim	tip	nip	pin	hit
him	hip	his	sit	pip	

By teaching another vowel, your list will increase by about eight words. Don't introduce *e* straight after *i* because these two sounds tend to be confused. It's better to teach *u* or *o* next. Concentrate on the most useful letters. I suggest teaching *b*, *c*, *d*, *l*, *r* and *o* and *u* next. Then perhaps *f*, *g*, *j*, *k*, *w*, *v* and *e*, and lastly, *q*, *y*, *x* and *z*. Some children like to have a small *u* put into their alphabet rainbow next to the *q* so that they won't forget that *u* always follows *q*.

If you have photocopied the top part of Chart 1, the alphabet in a rainbow shape, and stuck it into your child's exercise book, you can highlight each letter as you teach the

Chart 1   15

sound. This allows both of you to see which letters have been taught and is a very quick guide for you when you want to build words. You can see at a glance which letters you can use, and which you can't.

A word of warning. Many people, including some teachers, make the sound of a letter as if it included a short *ŭ*. For example, the sound of *b* is often pronounced *bu*, like the word *bus* without the *s*. It is much easier to say *bu cu du*, instead of the very short sounds *b c d*, but please don't. Problems arise when children start to string the sounds together – *bu i gu* tends to get made into *bigger* instead of *big*. I once taught a little boy who was building up the word *bug* and he produced a word that is not written in polite books! So please, although it is more difficult, make the sounds as clipped and short as you can.

As soon as you start building sentences, you will need a set of cards for the capital letters. They are on page 112. When you introduce capital letters ask your child to match the lower case letters to the capitals and point out that all capital letters are the same size as tall letters like *h* or *k*, and that they never have 'tails' hanging down below the line.

At the bottom of pages 109 and 111 there are some empty squares. Use these for spaces between words when your pupil is building sentences.

Sorting out *b* and *d*

The consonants *b* and *d* are very often confused, so teach one of them early and the other one later after several other letters have been learnt. This separation helps some children. In spite of this many children still confuse them. Here are four ways of helping to sort out *b*s and *d*s. Discuss them with your pupil and let him choose the one that he thinks will help him. You and he may even think of a new way that works for him.

1. Draw a bed using the word *bed*. If your child can visualise this picture, as well as read the word, it may help him.

2. Hold up both hands in front of you, with fingers pointing upwards and thumbs towards you. Make two rings with your forefingers and thumbs, keeping the other fingers straight. Starting at the left, as you would do when reading, imagine the first four letters of the alphabet. Your fingers make the *b* and *d*.

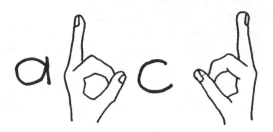

3. The words *bat* and *ball* begin with *b*. Starting at the left once more, think of a cricket bat and a ball. Together they make the shape of *b*.

4. Think of capital B when you write *b*, but lift your pencil off the paper when you make the top curve.

Building words (1)

There are two methods of building words; both are useful. I prefer the first method because it is reliable even when the pupil has to tackle very difficult words. Later I will explain how this technique is applied to longer words but for the moment I will show how a simple word like *hat* should be built when reading.

1. Cover up the *a* and *t* with your finger or piece of paper. The pupil has to make the sound of *h* out loud.
2. Move the cover along so that *h* and *a* can be seen. The pupil will probably say the sound of *a* out loud. At this point it is important to pause until the pupil can combine the sounds of *h* and *a* to say *ha*.
3. Remove the cover altogether. It should be fairly easy to combine *ha* and *t* to make *hat*.

This may seem complicated, but if the pupil builds like this at the early stages, the process will be automatic by the time he has to tackle more difficult words. If you are using the cards with individual letters on them, it is a good idea to put them down one at a time so that the pupil must build up a word in the way that I have described. Some pupils like to guess what the final letter of a word will be. For example, is *ha* going to become *ham* or *hat*?

Chart 1   17

Rhyming

The second method of building, which has recently become popular again, uses rhyming. If you take *an* and put different letters in front of it you will develop a list of rhyming words. I have also used *in, op* and *et* below. You could try other groups of letters.

an	in	op	et	
ban	bin	cop	bet	set
can	din	hop	get	vet
fan	fin	mop	jet	wet
man	pin	pop	let	
pan	sin	top	met	
ran	tin		net	
tan	win		pet	
van			yet	

Some children like rhyming. They get a lot of fun out of it, and will probably start to make up their own little poems. These children love the Dr. Seuss books such as *The Cat in a Hat*, published by Collins. Other children have no sense of rhyme and simply feel confused. I introduce rhyming as a game and only use it if the pupil enjoys it.

Jam Sandwich words

Start building words as soon as a few sounds are learnt. The first words I build are Jam Sandwich words. I will explain. If you have made letter cards using white cards for the consonants and red cards for the vowels, you will find that when you use the cards to make words, like those in the list below, you will have a pattern, white-red-white, for each word. The red vowel in the middle is the 'jam' in the sandwich.

a	e	i	o	u
sad	jet	pig	hot	bug
fat	den	bin	dog	cut
jam	red	fit	top	gun
van	leg	rib	nod	mud
tap	wet	zip	box	sun
bag	yes	six	jog	jug

Of course, you can start making your own Jam Sandwich words. The child can write them in his exercise book, arranged in five columns according to the vowels in the middle of the word, like the lists above. Don't make the lists too long at first; you can always add to them later if you need to. When you have made a few words, working together, the teacher should make a neat copy in the hard-backed book. It will look something like the lists above. Remember to leave several pages empty at the front of the book for the Contents, which in this case will start with, 'Page 1 Jam Sandwich Words'.

Other easy phonic words

Not all simple, regular words are Jam Sandwiches. Words like *it* and *up* are also phonic and can be built. They are very useful but don't fit into the consonant-vowel-consonant pattern. Here are some more.

an	at	in	if	us	on	is	and

As soon as the pupil is confident about the letters he has learnt, and can read simple words using these letters, ask him to build some of the words with the letter cards, if possible without looking at the lists.

Once a child begins to build simple words, everything begins to snowball. Adding only one more letter sound can dramatically increase the number of words he can build, read and write.

Making simple sentences and introducing a few 'Look and Say' words

The next step is to make simple sentences such as, *Ben cut his leg*, or *The dog is fat*. It is important to start this as early as possible. Use a capital letter at the beginning of each sentence and a full stop at the end. There is a card with a full stop on page 111. A list of Jam Sandwich names is given below to help you when you make up simple sentences.

Bob	Ben	Pat	Pam	Dan	Ron	Sam
Jim	Ken	Len	Tim	Meg	Ted	Tom

As soon as you start to make sentences you will find that you need some irregular words. Keep the number of these 'Look and Say' words to a minimum and make a flash card for each one. When you find you need some 'Look and Say' words that are not in my selection, you can easily make your own by using the Blank 'cards' on page 114. Here are a few irregular words that you will probably want quite soon, and there are more in Appendix 2 on page 96.

I	he	said	be	go
to	was	all	he	no
of	my	are	me	so
the	you	for	we	see

Chart 1   19

I must explain about this last word, *see*. Strictly speaking, it is regular, but at this point in learning to read, the pupil will not have learnt the sound made by *ee*. Therefore, I introduce it as a 'Look and Say' word.

Even when a pupil is trying to read Irregular words, knowing the sounds of the alphabet is a great help. The sound of the first letter gives a valuable clue to the word.

The sentences below use Jam Sandwich words, together with a few 'Look and Say' words. These are just examples. It is much better for you and your pupil to make your own.

Sam can fix his zip.

Pam has a pot of red jam.

Tom had fun on the top of the bus.

Jim has a big red van.

Put the bag in the bin.

The cat sat in the hot sun.

The big dog ran to the man.

Use the cards with single letters on them to build all the regular words. When you need an irregular word, which can't be built, make a flash card with the complete word on it. I have given you some more irregular 'Look and Say' words on page 96. Emphasise that a sentence must have a capital letter at the beginning and a full stop at the end and use space cards between words. Your sentence will look like this.

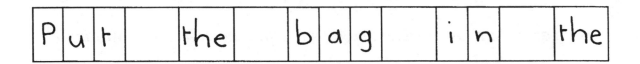

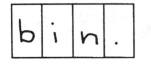

Making sentences in this way will take considerable time and effort. Show that you appreciate this by copying the sentences into your pupil's exercise book. Then you can look back on what has been achieved and use them for reading practice. The sentences don't always have to be sensible. Your pupil may prefer to write *Put the man in the bin.*

If a child is keen to make up a sentence that includes a word which is far beyond his ability, such as *aeroplane, tractor, space-ship, Christmas* or *birthday*, don't cramp his style. Simply supply the word as a 'Look and Say' word. He will probably always recognise it because it will have special significance for him. It will be much longer than all the other words that he is reading and writing at this stage, and every time he reads this long, difficult word it will boost his morale.

Three activities to practise simple words

It is important to link children's reading to 'real life' as soon as possible. Take a magazine or newspaper and ask your child to look at the headlines and see if he can find a particular word like *the* or *win*. Glancing quickly at my local newspaper I can see *at, on, net, sun, in, but, big,* and *his*. All these words, except *the*, are regular. Your pupil could take a felt-tip pen, ring all the words he can read and count how many he rings each time. Trying to improve his score will encourage him to watch out for words he can read. This activity, which I call **Making a Mess of the Newspaper**, also gives practice in coping with different sizes and styles of print.

Young children often like to draw pictures. If a simple sentence, like *The dog is fat*, is written at the top of a page, then the pupil can use the rest of the page to draw a picture showing what the sentence is about. In order to draw a good picture, the pupil has to understand the sentence and include a suitable setting. Discussing possibilities gives practice in putting ideas into words. You will soon find that silly sentences lead to funny pictures.

Sometimes young pupils like to play another game I have invented. I call it **Find the Hidden Word.** The teacher chooses three of the picture cards, so that when the child writes down the initial letters of the pictures, or chooses the matching letter cards, he will discover the hidden word. Here are some examples.

sock   umbrella   numbers

s u n

rabbit   egg   door

r e d

balloon   apple   tree

b a t

windmill   egg   tree

w e t

If he can read the word he has made, he scores a point or perhaps wins a Smarty. Later, in a more difficult version of the game, the child chooses three pictures and the teacher

Chart 1   21

writes the initial letters. The pupil scores if the letters make a correct word.

The red borders around the vowel pictures once more reinforce the fact that every word has to have a vowel.

When a child can build and pronounce, or build and write, simple words, he is reading and writing. He has started to crack the code and use it.

Section 2 Unexpected Sounds

The Unexpected Sounds are in the middle part of Chart 1 which is on page 106. They are usually called consonant digraphs, which simply means two consonants combining to represent one sound. I prefer to call them Unexpected Sounds.

If you photocopied Chart 1 and cut it into sections, the middle section can now be stuck into the exercise book. Once more, you can highlight the boxes as the sounds are learnt.

Imagine that you are a child who has just learnt the sounds of all the letters. Then you see the word *chip*, and try to build it. It is impossible, if you use the sounds of the alphabet that you have just learnt. The first two letters will defeat you. You can't put the *c* sound and the *h* sound together to make the first sound of *chip*. When *c* and *h* come together they make a new and completely *Unexpected* Sound and the pupil has to look out for this.

The Unexpected Sounds are:

ch as in *ch*ip or ri*ch*	*wh-* as in *wh*en	*-ng* as in si*ng*
sh as in *sh*op or fi*sh*	*qu-* as in *qu*id	*-nk* as in ba*nk*
th as in *th*in or wi*th*		

As you can see, some Unexpected Sounds can come at the beginnings or at the ends of words, and I do not use a dash with these. The dash after *wh* and *qu* shows that other letters follow. Similarly, the dash before *ng* and *nk* shows that other letters come in front of these.

The Unexpected Sounds *-ng* and *-nk* are much easier to pronounce if you put a vowel in front of them, for example, *-ang*, *-ing*, *-ung*, and *-ank*, *-ink*, *-unk*.

All the Unexpected Sounds are very common, so I teach them straight after the single letter sounds have been learnt. Here are a few more simple words that include them.

ch		*sh*		*th*	
chat	much	shot	rush	that	path
chop		shut	wish	than	moth
chin		shed	push	them	bath
		ship			

wh-	*qu-*	*-ng*		*-nk*	
whip	quit	bang	long	ink	bunk
		ring	lung	tank	junk
		king	hang	pink	sank
		wing	sang	sink	wink
		song			

When you make neat lists in the pupil's hard-backed book use a double spread so that you have plenty of room for seven columns. Number the pages and add them to the Contents at the front of the book.

Building words (2)

When building words, never separate the two letters of an Unexpected Sound. Make cards for them using page 113, and add them to the cards with single letters. If you do this, the Unexpected Sounds can't be separated when you are building words. Build *chip* and *rich* like this.

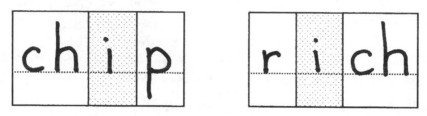

Use words with Unexpected Sounds in sentences as soon as you can. Try to keep to words that the child can build but, when necessary, you can supply words that are too difficult. In these two sentences I have emphasised the words that the pupil will probably need help with.

I can *play* with *my* ship in the bath.

The *queen likes* long thin chips.

Your cards will look like this:

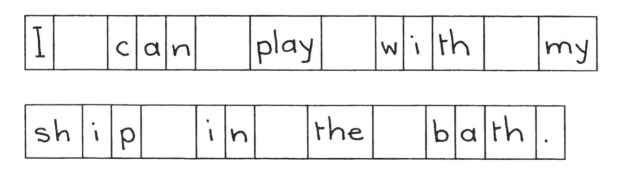

Chart 1   23

The		queen		likes		l	o	ng

th	i	n		ch	i	p	s	.

When you have made a sentence, write it out in the child's exercise book. You can highlight the new sounds you are practising or underline them with a bright colour. In the first sentence you would pick out *th* and *sh*. In the second sentence you would mark *qu-*, *-ng*, *th-* and *ch*. By this stage you may feel that you don't want to bother with blank cards to separate words. That's fine as long as there are always good big spaces to make sure that words don't run together.

Section 3 Blends

Now look at the bottom section of Chart 1 on page 106. It shows the commonest Blends. The letters in a Blend make exactly the same sound as the single letters of the alphabet. The two sounds simply flow together like food in a blender. Think of *fr* in *frog* or *-mp* in *jump*.

You will see from Chart 1 that there are three kinds of Blends:

- Two-letter Blends found at the beginnings of words.
- Two-letter Blends found at the ends of words.
- Three-letter Blends found at the beginnings of words.

I have included *sp* and *st* twice because they are common both as beginnings and endings of words. Like Unexpected Sounds, Blends are made up entirely of consonants. Here are a few sentences using the three kinds of Blends.

The dog can snap the twig.	*sn*	*tw*	
Push the plug in.	*pl*		
Bob has a drum and a flag.	*dr*	*fl*	
The lift went fast.	*-ft*	*-nt*	*-st*
The slug is on the plant.	*sl*	*pl*	*-nt*
The thrush has a nest in the bush.	*thr*	*-st*	
I must scrub the sink.	*-st*	*scr*	*nk*
The raft will drift.	*-ft*	*dr*	*-ft*
I was glad to go to the golf club.	*gl-*	*cl-*	

When you are making up sentences it helps to have a good selection of words to choose from, so here are more words with Blends.

crab	crisp	drop	drip	flat	flop	from	glad
grip	grin	grub	grab	plan	skin	skip	skid
slip	slim	spot	stop	stem	swim	swam	trap
trip	twin	act	gift	left	soft	milk	silk
belt	felt	lamp	camp	bump	end	land	send
stand	hand	grand	spend	mend	ant	bent	tent
best	lost	rest	west	last	test	list	rust
twist	scrap	split	shrimp	splash	spring	string	strong

Some children find Blends quite simple, but others have trouble with them and need lots of practice. Reading them doesn't normally give as much trouble as writing them. Some children have difficulty in hearing the *r* in *frog* or the *m* in *jump* when they try to convert sounds into writing. In some parts of the country, the *r* is not clearly pronounced, but in other places it is sounded very clearly and rolled impressively.

Make short lists of a few words with Blends in the hard-backed book, if you think your child needs them. You may decide to list only end Blends or three-letter Blends.

Two activities for practising Blends

Blends can be practised without reading or writing. All you have to do is *listen*. Pupils are surprised when I tell them that their ears can help them to spell. Here's a game that you could play during a car journey. Think of a word that starts with a Blend. Say the *sound* of the Blend, not the names of the letters, and give a clue. For example, you may think of *blue*, say *bl* and give the clue 'a colour'. If the other person gets the answer (either *blue* or *black* would be correct) it's their turn next. The clues can be more difficult, for example,

Blend	Clue	Answer
dr	an insect	dragonfly
gr	a big smile	grin
cr	a seashore creature	crab

Keep the game moving quickly by making it fairly easy. If the pupil fails too often or has to struggle too long, all the fun goes and he won't want to play the game. Some children need the help of word lists when it's their turn to give the teacher a clue. By the way, children's dictionaries are very handy for finding words that *start* with Blends.

The next idea helps with reading and encourages the child to recognise final Blends. The teacher writes out whole words, and the pupil has to underline or highlight the

Chart 1   25

Blends. The teacher then reads out most of the word slowly and the pupil makes the sound of the highlighted Blend at the right time to complete the word. Start with simple words like *sand* and *raft*. Older pupils can try longer words, such as *remind, invent* and *interest*.

Incidentally, did you spot that the word *blend* has two Blends?

Building words (3)

Building words with Blends is not very different from building Jam Sandwich words. It doesn't matter if the child separates a Blend as long as he can run it together again. When words have Blends and Unexpected Sounds, remember not to separate the letters of the Unexpected Sounds. For example, *crash* can be built in two ways,

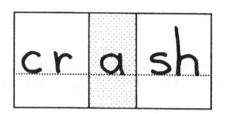 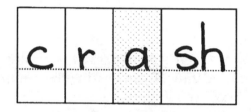

Again, rhyming is very useful. Put different vowels in front of a Blend and see what you can make. Here are some examples using the blend *-mp*.

-amp	-emp	-imp	-omp	-ump
camp		limp		jump
damp		chimp		bump
lamp				thump
stamp				plump

There are some words with *-emp* and *-omp* but they are not very useful. Don't be tempted to list words like *hemp*. The pupil has enough on his plate coping with the words he really needs.

If you have cut Chart 1 into three pieces, and stuck these into his exercise book, you can now make a new photocopy of the complete Chart and glue it into the front of his hard-backed book where you can both refer to it easily.

Conclusion

By the time a pupil has learnt everything on Chart 1 he should know:

- the sounds of the letters of the alphabet (and perhaps their names as well);
- the difference between small and capital letters and that we use capital letters to begin sentences and people's names;

- which letters are vowels, and that every word should have at least one;
- the Unexpected Sounds like *ch*, *sh*, etc.;
- the common Blends;
- some irregular 'Look and Say' words.

At this point the pupil will be able to read and write thousands of words and enjoy story books that use very simple vocabularies. Mum or Dad may have to step in to help with any difficult words that crop up, but his confidence will have grown and he will be starting to make sense of the whole business of reading and writing. Pause for a while, consider how much has been achieved and congratulate each other. You are now ready to start Chart 2 but before doing so I'd like you, the parent or teacher, to try something.

Can you spot the Unexpected Sounds and Blends?

Put yourself in the position of a child who has mastered Chart 1 but knows nothing else about reading and spelling. Look at the following sentences. Using two colours, mark the Blends in one colour and the Unexpected Sounds in the other. Try it first without any help. If you get muddled or find it too difficult (and adults often do) use Chart 1 to help you. When you finish you should have made 33 marks – 14 for Unexpected Sounds and 19 for Blends. It's easier to do the Unexpected Sounds first, and then go through the sentences again looking for Blends. I will do a sentence to give you an example, with the Unexpected Sounds underlined once, and the Blends underlined twice, and then you can try the others.

The strong man can lift the big box.

The <u>strong</u> man can li<u>ft</u> <u>the</u> big box.

Put <u>the</u> re<u>st</u> of <u>the</u> ju<u>nk</u> on <u>the</u> top <u>step</u>.

<u>Glen</u>da <u>spilt</u> the mi<u>lk</u>.

<u>Frank</u> is <u>bringing</u> a wet <u>cloth</u>.

<u>The</u> <u>frog</u> can ju<u>mp</u> a<u>nd</u> <u>splash</u> a<u>nd</u> swim.

Dad will get fi<u>sh</u> a<u>nd</u> <u>ch</u>ips.

<u>When</u> will Tim le<u>nd</u> me a <u>quid</u>?

To check the answers, turn to page 103. If you have marked 20 sounds correctly, you have done quite well. Often people who can read perfectly well find it very difficult. It just goes to show how hard it is to put ourselves into the position of the child we are trying to help.

Chart 1   27

Chart 2

Introduction

Chart 2 is much more challenging than Chart 1, but please don't let that put you off. **Even if you don't complete Chart 2, whatever you manage to do will be a help,** and you may find that once you get started, it's not as bad as it looks.

Having said that, I would hesitate to take a young child, or one who is progressing very slowly, straight on to Chart 2. If you feel that your pupil will be overwhelmed by Chart 2, you can use my Intermediate Chart as a stepping stone. I explain about the Intermediate Chart in Appendix 1.

I must tell you that some of my pupils haven't completed Chart 2 for various good reasons. You may reach a stage where the child can't take in any more. A colleague told me about 'the wobbly shelf theory'. This is how it goes. There is only so much that you can pile onto a shelf. If you overload it by just one thing, then the whole shelf will start to wobble. If you persist and add yet another item, then the whole lot will collapse in confusion. Teaching is just like this. Watch out for the warning wobble! It may be time to pause, revise and consolidate what has been taught and then consider whether or not to continue with new work. Sometimes a child will need a good long gap, especially if he is young, to practise using the letter combinations that he has been taught, before he is ready for more new work.

Sometimes one of my pupils feels that he is able to cope reasonably well with his school work, even though we still have some empty boxes on his Chart 2. When this happens I give him a completed copy of Chart 2, like the one on page 116, together with my Keywords Chart, which you can see on page 117, and we go through some of the sounds that he has not been taught, to see if he can work them out from the Keywords. By this stage, intelligent youngsters can often work out the correct sounds from the Keywords. Applying this knowledge to other words is not so easy.

I once taught an intelligent, well-motivated adult who preferred to go ahead by himself, as soon as he was happy with the method and routine I was using and had some good phonic word lists. Working like this takes a lot of determination and a child who attempts it will need lots of encouragement and occasionally some help too.

Whatever your reason for stopping regular sessions, make it clear that it is always possible to pick up where you left off. One of my pupils phoned me after a gap of four years and asked for more lessons. He had matured considerably and said that his weak spelling was now holding him back and causing him embarrassment.

However, these considerations won't be arising yet. Let's start from the point when you have decided that your pupil is ready to start Chart 2. If you are only assuming that your pupil knows the sounds on Chart 1, and haven't checked that he does, I advise you to run through Chart 1 very quickly to make absolutely sure that all the simplest steps in spelling and reading really have been learnt. You can do this by using the cards showing the single letters of the alphabet, the Unexpected Sounds and the Blends. First, present the cards and have the pupil make the sounds, and then *you* make the sounds and see if he can select the correct card. You could also give him a short spelling test based on the sounds on Chart 1.

Chart 2, which is mostly vowel combinations, is much more difficult work. It will take a long time to learn all the sounds represented on it and you don't want to be constantly backtracking to teach the earlier work on Chart 1.

Explanation of Chart 2 and two types of boxes

There are three versions of Chart 2. The one I show to the pupil is the Blank one, which is on page 115. Look at it now. What do you notice? 'Lots of squares', is the usual answer. I call them *boxes*. Are the boxes all the same? No, some boxes are divided into smaller boxes, others are not. Here are examples of the two types of boxes, and some words that include the sounds in them. You will find these completed boxes on the Chart 2 Guide on page 116. They are numbered 6 and 16.

a – e	game
ai	rain
– ay	day

wr	wrong
kn	knife
– mb	lamb
gu	guess

The first box has three groups of letters that make exactly the same sound. Consequently they are all in one big box. The second box contains groups of letters that make different sounds, and so they are put into their own separate little boxes. However, there is a reason why these little boxes are grouped together. In this case they all have silent letters. The *w* is silent in *wrong*, the *k* in *knit*, the *b* in *lamb*, and the *u* in *guess*.

If the pupil has just mastered the work on Chart 1, explain to him that his Blank Chart 2 will be filled in very gradually as he learns the sounds that fit into the boxes. Reassure him that he will not be rushed or overloaded. It will take a long time to fill in all the boxes. Tell him that the Chart will help him to remember the sounds he has learnt, when he needs them for his reading and writing. Stick this Blank Chart in the pupil's hard-backed book, at the very back, on the inside of the stiff cover.

There is a set of letter cards that correspond to Chart 2 on pages 119–22. Photocopy

Chart 2 29

them, cut them up and see if your child knows any of the sounds that they make. (You can work out the sounds from my Chart 2 – Keywords on page 117.) Many children know *oo* or *ee*. If your pupil knows the sound of a letter combination, write it on his Blank Chart 2 straight away, so that he gets credit for what he knows, and put that letter card with his other letter cards so that it is available for building words. Some children like to use letter cards during a spelling test to work out the correct order of the letters before writing down a word.

There is no set order for filling in the boxes, but I suggest one possible teaching order in a later section. Common sense will guide you to teach the easiest or most useful sounds first. As soon as a few boxes are filled, the Chart begins to be useful.

The Chart 2 Guide on page 116 is the completed version and is not for the pupil's use. It reminds the teacher where to enter the sounds on the Blank Chart.

Some teachers find it useful to pin up an A3 version of Chart 2 Guide as a poster. If you think that this would be useful, you can enlarge the A4 sheet on a photocopier.

Uses of Chart 2

The chart has three main uses.

1. The groups of letter combinations form a structure or pattern on the page which gradually becomes familiar to the pupil. For example, after a while he can recall what is at the top left or top right of the Chart. Peter Gardner, an educational psychologist writing in the Educational Section in the *Guardian* said, 'Dyslexic children are fairly unstructured people, and need a structure to hold on to'. Chart 2 provides a useful structure.

   Grouping the sounds into boxes makes a change from the more usual lists. Remember that different approaches suit different people, so if there is a difficulty, a new way of doing things may help. Sometimes I have found that the sounds on Chart 2 have been taught as completely separate items and the child has never realised that, for instance, *er*, *ir* and *ur* make the same sound. It has come as a revelation and relief to group them together. Somehow putting letter combinations that make the same sounds into one box seems to give the pupil more control over them.

   Connections between the boxes are important too. Boxes 1 and 2 are together because they both contain endings for the same type of word. There are strong links between Boxes 4 and 5. Box 4 is also related to Box 3. These links will become clear when I discuss the arrangement of the boxes in a later section.

2. The Chart is a memory aid and also helps with revision. By putting several letter combinations into one big box, the pupil can use one combination, whose sound he remembers, to remind himself of the sound of another group of letters whose sound he has forgotten. For example, if he knows the sound made by *a-e* as in *game*, he can work out the sound of *ai* in *wait*, because *a-e* and *ai* are in the same box.

   The Chart helps revision because it organises lots of letter combinations and spelling rules into a sensible order. The pupil can see at a glance what he has been taught and quickly check whether he can remember the sounds correctly. If his memory fails him and there is only one sound in that box, he can refer to his

Keyword Chart (which I explain on page 45) or look at his word list for that sound where he will find an easy word to help him work out the sound that has slipped his memory.

Undoubtedly the best way to revise is to use the Chart as much as possible. Perhaps the pupil could carry a smaller version or a folded copy tucked into his pocket for quick reference. There is a photocopiable A5 version on page 123.

An enormous amount of information is summarised and displayed on Chart 2. This single A4 page can help with the vast majority of English spelling. If a pupil learns to use the Chart he will cope reasonably well with whatever he wants to read or write.

3. As the Chart is being filled in, it is a record of progress for the teacher, the parent, and most important of all, for the pupil.

If a teacher has several pupils who are being taught individually, they will be progressing at different speeds and it will be difficult for her to remember what each pupil has been taught. By having her own copies of the pupils' Charts she can easily check the progress of each child. Of course if a group of children are being taught together, then one Chart will be enough for the whole group. When a child goes to a new teacher, the Chart quickly shows the new teacher which sounds have been taught to that child.

Parents find the chart useful too, particularly if the child is young. Mum or Dad can ask if another box has been filled in, and if so, what sound those letters make. The Chart is a good starting point to chat about the lessons, and also to show what progress is being made.

The pupil himself can also get an idea of his progress when he sees more and more boxes being filled.

There are a great many boxes to fill. Give plenty of praise and encouragement. Let him know that he is making good progress when only a few boxes are filled. Don't feel that a new box has to be filled in at every lesson. He will need pauses to re-cap on what has been taught. He should be happy and confident with his progress.

Arrangement of the boxes

Now let's look at Chart 2 Guide, which shows our most useful letter combinations. The Guide Chart on page 116 has numbers below the boxes to make it easier for you to follow what I am talking about. The Blank Chart that the pupil uses has no numbers.

I will explain the arrangement of the boxes as I work through them in numerical order, illustrating each sound with a word that you will find on Chart 2 Keywords. I must emphasise that this is *not* the order in which they should be taught. In the next section of this book I suggest an order for teaching, and I give lists of words and dictation sentences which use each sound.

Boxes 1 and 2 are together because they both contain endings for short words with short vowels. When I teach these sounds I outline these two boxes in red because these are the only two boxes on the chart that are linked with short vowels.

Box 1 has double endings that come straight after the vowel. I teach -*ck* as a double because, when you say the sounds of the alphabet, *c* and *k* make the same noise.

Chart 2   31

Examples of words that have these double endings are *cliff*, *shell*, *miss* and *sock*. Children often read these words easily but forget the double letters when writing.

Box 2 has two more endings for short words with short vowels. These endings have silent letters. We don't hear the *d* in *hedge*, or the *t* in *match*.

Boxes 3, 4 and 5 are connected and are grouped towards the top right corner of the Chart. They are linked because the vowels *e*, *i* and *y* soften *c* and *g*.

Box 3 contains *ke-* and *ki-*. We must use a *k* before an *e* or *i* if we want a hard sound. If we use a *c* it will be softened by the vowels that follow it, to make the sound *s*. Examples of *ke-* and *ki-* words are *kettle* and *kill*.

Box 4 has *c* followed by the three vowels which soften it. Examples are *central*, *city* and *cycle*. Notice how all these words sound as if they start with an *s*. *Cycle* is interesting because the second *c* is hard.

Box 5 shows *g* which is softened by the same three vowels, *e*, *i* and *y*. Examples of these words are *germ*, *giant* and *gym*. They all sound as if they start with *j*.

Boxes 6, 7, 8, 9 and 10 go right across the Chart. At the top of these boxes you will see the five vowels. They are now long vowels because they have the silent *e*, which I explain on page 34. Words that have this silent *e* are *game*, *Pete*, *time*, *home* and *tune*.

Box 6 has two other combinations that make the same sound as *a-e*. These are *ai* and *-ay*, which occur in *rain* and *day*.

Box 7 has *ee* and *ea* which make the same sounds as *e-e*. We find them in *tree* and *eat*.

Box 8 has three more combinations of letters that make the same sound as *i-e*. These are *ie*, *-igh* and *y*, which occur in *pie*, *fight* and *sky*. We usually have a *t* after *-igh*, so I have shown it in brackets.

Box 9 also has three more letter groups, *oe*, *oa* and *ow*, which all make the same sound as *o-e*. They are in *toe*, *boat* and *slow*.

Box 10 contains *-ue*, *oo* and *ew*, which make the same sound as *u-e*. Examples of these sounds are in words like *blue*, *moon* and *new*.

Boxes 11, 12 and 13, towards the left of the Chart, contain the five vowels, each one combined with an *r*. The three groups *er*, *ir* and *ur* all make the same sound and are therefore all in one box. The combination *er* is nearly always used as an ending, whereas *ir* and *ur* are not often at the end of a word. The sounds of *or* and *ar* are different.

Box 11 has the sounds *er*, *ir* and *ur*. Examples are *her*, *girl* and *burn*.

Box 12 has two other letter combinations that make the same sound as *or*. The words *pork*, *Paul* and *law* contain *or*, *au* and *aw*.

Box 13 contains the *ar* sound. An easy word is *car*.

Box 14 has the letter combinations *oi-* and *-oy*, which come in words like *oil* and *boy*.

Box 15 contains *ou* and *ow*. We see the sound *ou* in words like *out*. Did you notice that we already have the other sound *ow* in Box 9? The reason that *ow* is in two boxes is that it can make two sounds. It can make the sound in *owl* as well as the sound in *slow*.

Box 16 is a divided box that contains some common combinations with silent letters. We see *wr-* in *wrong*, *kn-* in *knife*, *-mb* in *lamb*, and *gu* in *guess*.

Box 17 is another divided box. It has two groups of letters where the *i* is long. Examples are *kind* and *child*.

Box 18 is a divided box. It contains six words that are very useful because they appear within longer words. For example, *all* comes in *ball*, *old* in *gold*, *ace* in *face*, *ice* in *mice*, *age* in *page*, and *other* in *mother*.

Box 19 has *-air* and *-are* which we see in the words *chair* and *spare*.

Box 20 contains two long strings of letters that make the same sound and almost look alike. We get *aught* in *taught* and *ought* in *bought*.

Box 21 This odd group of letters, *-alk*, comes in *talk*.

Box 22 The question marks in this box indicate that this group of letters is very puzzling. It can make many different sounds and five of these sounds are found in common words. I will explain more about this later, but if you want to work out the five sounds that I am thinking of, try to work them out from *though*, *through*, *plough*, *cough* and *tough*.

Box 23 shows another odd group of letters, but the good news is that there are only three words that use them, *could*, *would* and *should*.

Box 24 has two sounds that, strictly speaking, should have been included in the Unexpected Sounds on Chart 1, but they are taught at a much later stage than the rest of Chart 1, so I have included them here. They are used in the words *phone* and *chemist*.

Box 25 has some very useful endings, *-le* appears in *little*, *-ture* in *picture*, and *-tion* in *station*.

Box 26 is in the same column as Box 7 because the combination *ea* is in both. In Box 26 it has (ĕ) after it to remind the pupil that it is a short sound. We see it in words like *head*.

Box 27 is under Box 8 for the same reason. They both have *-y* in them. The letter in Box 27 has (ĭ) after it to indicate a short vowel. This sound is a very common ending on words like *funny*.

Box 28 contains the combinations *wa* and *wo*, which have odd pronunciations. If you think carefully about the sound of *wash*, you will realise that the *wa* makes the sound of *wo*. Similarly the *wo* in *wolf* makes a *wu* sound. On the Chart the letters you *see* are given first and the sound you *hear* is in brackets.

At the bottom of the Chart are two sets of longer boxes. The boxes on the left refer to two very useful spelling rules. The boxes on the right are all concerned with forming plurals.

Chart 2 33

Suggested order of teaching the letter combinations on Chart 2, with revision exercises, spelling rules, etc.

No two teachers will teach the sounds on Chart 2 in the same order. However, there is broad agreement about which sounds a child needs first. I am going to suggest one possible teaching order and there is a photocopiable checklist in the same order on page 118. You will see that sometimes I teach a comparatively easy sound straight after a difficult one. I find that this gives the child a boost.

a-e e-e i-e o-e u-e Boxes 6, 7, 8, 9 and 10

In some schools the final *e* on these sounds is called 'silent e'. Other schools call it 'lazy e', or 'magic e'. I tend to call it 'silent', but let your pupil decide which name he likes.

The words that use the 'silent e' are a natural development from the Jam Sandwich words. If you are teaching a young child or someone who needs to progress very slowly, teach only one of these five sounds in a session. Start with a Jam Sandwich word, such as *hat*, put on a 'silent e' and explain that the word has changed completely and now says *hate*. You might like to make the sentence, '*I hate that hat*'.

The 'silent e' makes the vowels say their names which, as you remember, are quite different from the short sounds that we have been using up to now. The *names* of the letters *a, e, i, o* and *u*, are *long* vowel sounds. I explain the difference between long and short vowel sounds by showing that you can make a long vowel sound very, very long. It's like a piece of elastic. You can stretch it. Let's take *a* as an example. Take a deep breath and make the long *a* sound (*ā*) that comes in the middle of *name*. You can keep it going as long as your breath lasts. On the other hand, you cannot stretch the short *a* sound (*ă*) in the middle of *cat*. It's just impossible. Get the pupil to experiment in this way too. He will only appreciate the difference after he has tried it for himself. Often children start to distort the *ă* into *ar*, as in *car*, desperately trying to make it stretch. Remind them of the correct, clipped *ă* sound.

a-e Box 6

Here are some Jam Sandwich words with *ă* that can be changed into different, new words by adding a 'silent e'.

hat .. hate	tap .. tape	rat .. rate	mad .. made	mat .. mate

When your pupil has understood how the 'silent e' makes the vowel say its name, you can introduce other words that don't start as Jam Sandwich words. Below are some examples that I have separated into three groups; easy words in the first two columns, words with Unexpected Sounds in the third column, and words with Blends in the last two columns. Older or more advanced pupils will need to be aware of *a-e* in longer words, such as *demonstrate*, *hurricane* and *landscape*. I have made lists of more difficult words with *a-e, e-e, i-e, o-e* and *u-e* on page 38. Pick out some words from these lists if you feel that the words below are too easy for him.

name	cave	shave	brave	taste
gave	lane	whale	spade	waste
late	Kate	shape	plate	paste
came	Dave	shade	stale	
gate	Jane	shame	slate	
wave		bathe	scrape	

All the sounds on Chart 2 are on pages 119–22 for you to photocopy. Explain that the *a-e* card needs a space so that we can fit in single letters when we build words. The space is shown with a little dash. Build words like this.

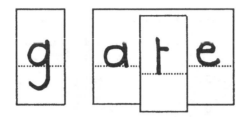

When you put a letter into the gap in the *a-e* card, it's easy to add different letters at the beginning and make a list of rhyming words. This idea can be used with many other letter combinations too, and it gives good practice in using the new sound. Be careful to avoid mistakes like *kame* and *wate*. When you check through the Unexpected Sounds and Blends on Chart 1, you will find more possibilities, like *flame*, *skate* and *shave*.

-ame	*-ate*	*-ave*
came	date	cave
game	gate	Dave
lame	hate	gave
name	Kate	save
same	late	wave
tame	mate	

When you want to underline the sound *a-e* in words like *gate*, use a curved line instead of a straight one, because you don't want to include the *t*. It should look like this.

gate   not   gate

When you have taught *a-e*, enter it at the top of Box 6 on the Blank Chart, which you should have stuck onto the inside of the back cover of the pupil's hard-backed book. Let the child help you to choose some *a-e* words to make a list in the main part of the hard-

Chart 2   35

backed book. Enter *a-e* in the Contents at the front of the book together with the page number. This means that *a-e* should now appear in three places in the hard-backed book.

- at the back on Chart 2
- at the top of a word list
- in the Contents at the front

Some children like to make up nonsense words and this can be a good way of checking that they really know their sounds. Other children hate nonsense words and think that they are a complete waste of time. Here are a few examples using *a-e*. See if your pupil likes them.

vape	jate	zame	quabe	lafe	wabe

I often dictate simple sentences to practise the sounds that I have recently taught. Remember you may have to give help with 'Look and Say' words. If you can make up your own sentences, which have more meaning for your pupil, they will be better than the ones I give below. When the dictation is finished, ask the child to highlight the special sound that you have been practising.

Dictation sentences

His name is Dave.
The tame cub came to the gate.
I made Dad mad.
My mate was late for the game but he made a good save.

It is safe to go into the cave.
Jane gave a grape to Kate.
Frank came to see the whale.

i-e Box 8

I suggest that you teach *i-e* next. It's a very common sound. Here are some Jam Sandwich words that can be made into new words, followed by more *i-e* words.

win .... wine	bit .... bite	hid .... hide	fin .... fine
rip .... ripe	pin .... pine	rid .... ride	pip .... pipe

wise	line	white	smile	drive
file	five	chime	bride	prize
mile	wipe	shine	spine	glide
fire	vile	quite	slime	crime
time	size	while	grime	twine
mine	wide		stripe	Clive
wire	nine			
dive	tide			

Please don't think that you must work through all these word lists slavishly. I am giving fairly long lists so that you have a good selection of words to choose from. It is difficult to produce the right kind of words straight off the top of your head.

Dictation sentences

It is not wise to drive fast.

That was a vile crime.

Do not cross the wide white line.

He will slide and slip in the slime.

Five plums are quite ripe.

Clive will dine with white wine.

She ran a mile and got the prize.

The plane can dive and glide.

o-e Box 9

First a few Jam Sandwich words that can be changed into different words by adding a 'silent e' and then lists of other *o-e* words.

hop .... hope   cod .... code   not .... note   rob .... robe

home	bone		those		stone
nose	tone		chose		froze
rope	hole				drove
owe	pole				close
Rose	hose				stole

Dictation sentences

She stole the rose.

He broke the bone in his nose.

The Pope has a home in Rome.

Push the stone with a pole.

I hope Rose drove home with the note.

The mole dug a hole.

u-e Box 10

Once more some Jam Sandwich words with a short *ŭ* sound that can be changed by the 'silent e', followed by other *u-e* words. There are not so many short words with this sound, but it is used quite often in longer words which you will find on page 38.

tub .... tube   cut .... cute   us .... use   cub .... cube

rule	tune	mule	rude		prune
fuse	cure	pure	June		flute

Dictation sentences

Use the flute to play a tune.

It is a rule not to prune the roses in June.

June will mend the fuse.

Chart 2 37

e-e Box 7

Very few easy words have this combination, but I teach it at this early stage because it fits in with the general rule about the 'silent e' changing the short vowels into long ones. The only simple Jam Sandwich word in this group is *them* changing to *theme*. I warn my pupils that we don't use this sound much until we get to longer words. Here are a few short words.

| here | Pete | Eve | mere | these |

Dictation sentence
Here is Pete with Eve.

Longer words using *a-e*, *e-e*, *i-e*, *o-e* and *u-e*

If you are teaching an older or more advanced pupil, he will need to practise longer words. After checking that he understands the effect of the 'silent e' ask him to read the following words, which have *a-e*, *e-e*, *i-e*, *o-e* and *u-e* mixed up. When he has read the words get him to mark the sounds that include the 'silent e'.

investigate	indicate	manure	extreme
insecure	complete	entire	dispose
escape	compose	rebate	improvise
illustrate	demonstrate	contemplate	atmosphere
inspire	empire	severe	athlete
decompose	manicure	include	exclude

-ff, -ll, -ss and -ck Box 1

This box, which I outline in red, contains double endings for short words with short vowels, and the double endings come immediately after the vowel. I include -ck as a double because the c and k both make the same sound when children first learn the alphabet, as you can hear in *cat* and *kitten*. Words never end with two cs or two ks. We use one of each. Some pupils can cope with learning all four double endings together, others have to learn them one at a time. But before I give you lists of words with these endings, I would like to talk about syllables.

Syllables

You can count syllables by clapping. *Con-grat-u-late* has four claps, therefore four syllables. *Beautiful* has three. Practise counting syllables in both long and short words. Emphasise that it is not the *look* of a word that matters. For example, *strength* has eight letters but is only one syllable, whereas *radio* has five letters and has three syllables. It divides *ra / di / o*. If you write long words on slips of paper your pupil can cut them up into syllables, and then copy them perhaps using a different colour for each syllable. Older pupils may not want to clap. They can count syllables on their fingers.

One more point about syllables, each syllable must have at least one vowel. Even *I* and *a*, which are our shortest words, have a vowel, don't they? You may have a pupil who quite rightly divides *funny* into two syllables, and then wonders why the second syllable doesn't have a vowel. If so you will have to explain about *y* sometimes being a vowel and sometimes a consonant. (See page 53.) Normally I explain about this later, but you can teach it now if it crops up.

-ff Box 1

There are not many words using *-ff*.

cliff	off	puff	sniff	stiff	fluff

-ll Box 1

The sound *-ll* is much more common. I have arranged these words according to their vowel.

bell	tell	hill	will	doll	full
fell	well	kill	ill		pull
hell	swell	bill	thrill		skull
sell	spell	fill	drill		bull
		pill	still		gull

-ss Box 1

Words ending in *-ss* are also common.

pass	mess	kiss	boss	fuss
grass	less	miss	cross	
class	dress		gloss	
brass	press			
glass	chess			

There are a few exceptions to the *-ss* rule, for example *yes*, *bus* and *gas*, but these don't normally give trouble.

Chart 2   39

-ck Box 1

The ending -ck is very common.

back	smack	neck	kick	stick	lock		luck
sack	snack	deck	sick	pick	rock		duck
pack	track	peck	lick	tick	sock		suck
black	stack		brick	click	clock		stuck
crack	slack		trick		block		truck
Jack							

Dictation sentences

The black pill did not make him well.
It made him sick.
Jack fell off the cliff and was ill.
Tell the man to lock his truck.

The clock is fast.
The duck will make a mess on the grass.
Kate will win the chess game.

If you are finding that your pupil does not like the sentences you are suggesting, get him to look at his word lists and make up his own. You will have to give more help with 'Look and Say' words, but that doesn't matter. It's better that he is writing something that gives him more pleasure.

Older pupils, who are using longer words, may be unsure about the end of a word like *pathetic*. The answer is that if a word ends in a *k* sound, and is more than one syllable, we use a *c* at the end. For example,

picnic magic Arctic terrific Atlantic Pacific

-ake / -ack   -ike / -ick   -oke / -ock   -uke / -uck

This is a very good time to revise long and short vowels. Many children mix *back* and *bake*, and frequently write words like *backe*. Tell your child that we always use *k* when the vowel is long. Here are some pairs of words and sentences for dictation.

back .... bake	lick .... like	cock .... coke	duck .... duke
tack .... take	pick .... pike	chock .... choke	luck .... Luke
shack .... shake	Mick .... Mike	block .... bloke	
snack .... snake		jock .... joke	
Jack .... Jake			

Tell your pupil he must get it right. No Duke will want to be called a duck!

Dictation sentences

The duke likes to see ducks on the lake.
Jock is a good bloke. He can take a joke.
Quick, pick up the sack and run.
Black smoke came from Mike's shack.

Make Jake bring the bike back.
Shake the dust off the back of your dress.
Do not choke. Drink the coke.

Adding endings to words (1) When to drop the final *e*

Children will very soon want to add endings (suffixes) to words. Words like *hope* that end in *e* give problems. We keep the final *e* when we write *hopes,* but drop it when we write *hoping.* There is a very good, simple rule to explain this.

If the ending starts with a vowel, drop the e.

Here are some examples adding *s, ed* and *ing.*

wave	joke	wipe	fire	cure
waves	jokes	wipes	fires	cures
waved	joked	wiped	fired	cured
waving	joking	wiping	firing	curing

Many children will tell you that when they want to write *liked,* they just need to add a *d.* Explain to them that really they are dropping the *e* from *like* and adding *ed.* I know it looks the same whichever way you do it, but if you get them used to using *ed* for something that happened in the past, it will avoid them writing things like *I cleand my bike,* or *He orderd chips.*

Later on, when your pupil is using more unusual endings like *-ly, -ment, -ful* and *-less,* that don't start with a vowel, the simple rule about dropping the *e* will still be very useful. Point out that the ending *-ful* has only one *l.*

completing	amusing	hating	caring
completely	amusement	hateful	careless

all old ace ice age other Box 18

These are little words that are often found inside longer words, so it's very useful to know them.

-all	-old	-ace	-ice	-age	-other
ball	gold	face	nice	page	mother
fall	fold	race	mice	wage	brother
call	cold	lace	rice	cage	another
hall	hold	space	dice	rage	smother
tall	sold	trace	price	stage	
wall	told	place	twice		
small			slice		
stall			spice		

Chart 2   41

You now have a lot of words on your lists and it would be better if you and your pupil made up your own dictation sentences. However, for those who find this difficult, I will continue to provide some.

Dictation sentences

Do small mice like cold rice with spice?   The vice will hold it in place.
The tall man on the stage had a nice face.
We have space for my mother, brother and one other.
If you run in the race you will get a big slice of ice cream.
Mother told us that she had sold the old cage for a good price.

ee ie oe ue   Boxes 7, 8, 9 and 10

Some pupils can learn all these sounds in one session. They are the same as *e-e*, *i-e*, *o-e* and *u-e*. All that has happened is that we have missed out the gap and pushed the letters together. When we have two vowels together, very often the *name* of the first one is the correct sound.

ee   Box 7

The sound *ee* may be already known because it is very common. Many years ago I learnt about Green Feet from Gill Cotterell and they have never failed to amuse everyone I have ever taught. This is what you do. First have a bath or shower. Then stand with both feet on a piece of plain paper and draw round your feet using a green pen. If you look at page 43 the rest is obvious, although the picture has been reduced. Arrange the words *feet*, *feel*, *green* and *heel* so that each foot has one *e*. Then fill in spaces with any *ee* words that are easy to illustrate, for example, *seed*, *leek* and *queen*.

When you make a list of *ee* words some of them need a note beside them because we have words that sound exactly the same but are spelt with *ea* and have different meanings. I delay teaching *ea* until later to reduce confusion. Here are more *ee* words.

keep	free	sweet	sheet	three
feed	teeth	wheel	street	meet (a friend)
tree	speed	sheep	speech	week (7 days)

Dictation sentences

Last week I went to meet Dad in Hill Street.   I can see a sheep under the beech tree.
Keep the speed down.   That car has three wheels.
If you want to keep your teeth eat less sweets.

e e

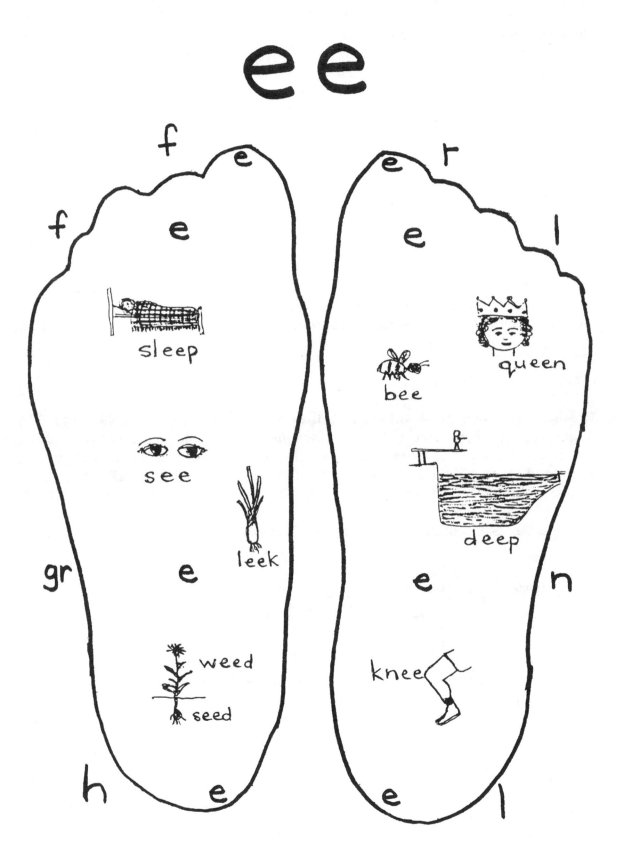

f f e e

gr e

h e

e r e l

e

queen
bee

deep

e n

knee

e l

sleep

see

leek

weed

seed

Chart 2 43

ie, *oe* and **ue** Boxes 8, 9 and 10.

There are not so many *ie*, *oe* and *ue* words.

pie	toe	blue	Sue	tissue
tie	hoe	true	value	avenue
die	Joe	glue	rescue	continue
lie		clue	statue	argue

You will see that I am now including some more difficult words for those pupils who need a challenge.

Dictation sentences

I will lie about his tie and tell him I like it.
She will die if she has the pie.
The statue at the end of the avenue held the clue.
They will continue to argue about the true value of the gold box.

Sue likes blue glue.
Joe cut his toe with the hoe.

Plurals (1) Adding *es*

Singular means one; plural means more than one. In most cases we make a plural by simply adding *s*. For example, *dog* changes to *dogs* and *brick* to *bricks*. However, this is not always the case. Think about the words *glass*, *church*, *dish* and *box*. If you say these words and try to add the sound *s*, you will find it doesn't work. We make an *uz* sound for these plurals. This is a very good example of how your ears can help you to spell.

glasses	churches	dishes	boxes
kisses	peaches	crashes	foxes
classes	beaches	bushes	taxes
crosses	branches	wishes	sexes
masses	lunches	brushes	mixes

You may have to help your pupil with *churches*, *peaches* and *beaches* because they haven't been taught *ur* and *ea* sounds yet. In spite of this little snag I like to teach *es* plurals at an early stage because most of the words that have an *es* plural are simple words.

Dictation sentences

The foxes ran into the bushes.
He had three crashes.
I like ripe peaches.

The old man gave him five wishes.
She put masses of dishes in the sink.
Pack the glasses in the boxes.

ar Box 13

This is a very straightforward sound. It occurs in easy words and, if you look at Chart 2, you will see that we have no other letter combination making the same sound, so there is no problem about when to use *ar*.

car	art	scar	cart	carpet
card	part	scarf	March	garden
bar	star	dark	sharp	harvest
bark	start	yard	shark	market
arm	far	park	smart	remark
harm	farm	hard	spark	Mark

Dictation sentences
Mark will park the car in the farm yard after dark.
Start to dig in this part of the garden.   Some sharks will not harm you.

Introducing Chart 2 Keywords

At this stage you will have filled in about twenty-two spaces on your pupil's Chart 2. He may be finding it a bit difficult to remember all the sounds that you have taught him. If so, he needs something to help him to work out the sounds when his memory fails him, and you are not sitting beside him. At this point I introduce a Keywords Chart to correspond with his Chart 2.

The Keywords Chart starts off as a Blank Chart 2 and it should be stuck at the back of the hard-backed book on the left page opposite his partially completed Chart 2. When you have done this, look at your pupil's word lists and let him choose one easy word from each list which you enter on his Keywords Chart, in the corresponding place. It is best if he chooses his own Keywords, because they must be words which he can read easily, if they are going to be effective Keywords. From now on, when necessary, he will be able to look straight across from one Chart to the other, and the words on the Keywords Chart will help his memory. For example, if he has forgotten what *ew* says, but he knows the word *new*, he can work out the *ew* sound and then read words like *flew* and *threw*.

You can see an example of a Keywords Chart with twenty-two places filled in on page 46, and I have included a Keywords Chart on page 117, as a guide only, not to be copied.

From now on, when you teach a new sound, there will be four places to enter that sound in the hard-backed book:

- on Chart 2 at the back of the book;
- at the top of the word list in the main part of the book;
- on the Keywords Chart at the back of the book, embedded in an easy word;
- in the Contents at the beginning of the book.

Chart 2 45

EXAMPLE OF CHART 2 KEYWORDS

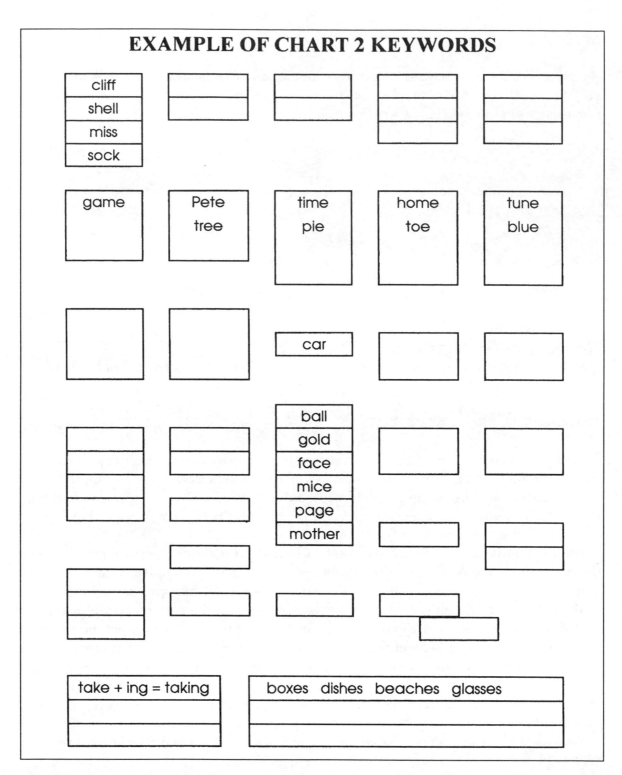

cliff				
shell				
miss				
sock				

game	Pete tree	time pie	home toe	tune blue

car

ball
gold
face
mice
page
mother

take + ing = taking	boxes dishes beaches glasses

oo *Box 10*

Again your pupil may know several words using this sound. Ask him to write any *oo* words that he can remember. If you suggest words like *moon, roof, spoon, boot* and *cool* he will probably be able to work them out, but be careful because there are some *oo* words that are pronounced differently in most parts of the country. They are in the last two columns.

			look	wood
room	poor	broom	look	wood
zoo	soon	stool	book	hood
zoom	noon	shoot	hook	good
too	food	tooth	cook	stood
root	tool	smooth	took	wool
fool	pool		shook	foot

You will probably find that your lips are pushed further forward when you say words like *room* and *zoo*, than when you say *book*.

Dictation sentences

We took the food into the cool room.
The old stool was made of smooth wood.
Soon we will be out of the wood and see the pool.

The poor fool took the broom away.
Look, this is a good book.

-ould Box 23

I teach this peculiar combination of letters early. It comes in only three words and most children learn to reel them off in one breath, 'Could, would, should'. You may have to chant 'o-u-l-d' over and over with your pupil before the letters come automatically, but it usually doesn't take long. Then they have another box on Chart 2 filled and can cope with three awkward words.

ai Box 6

This is another very common sound. It makes the same noise as *a-e*, which we did earlier. In order to help the pupil remember which of these two letter combinations to use, I ask him to draw a picture including as many of the things on this word list as he can.

rain	pain	train	snail	waiting
sail	paint	stain	trail	pail (bucket)
nail	rail	chain	waist	Gail
tail	railway	aid	Spain	Craig

If they can't remember whether to use *a-e* or *ai* the picture will help with many of the commonest words. If something is in the picture, it will have *ai*. One of my previous pupils has allowed me to reproduce his picture of *ai* words on page 48.

Chart 2   47

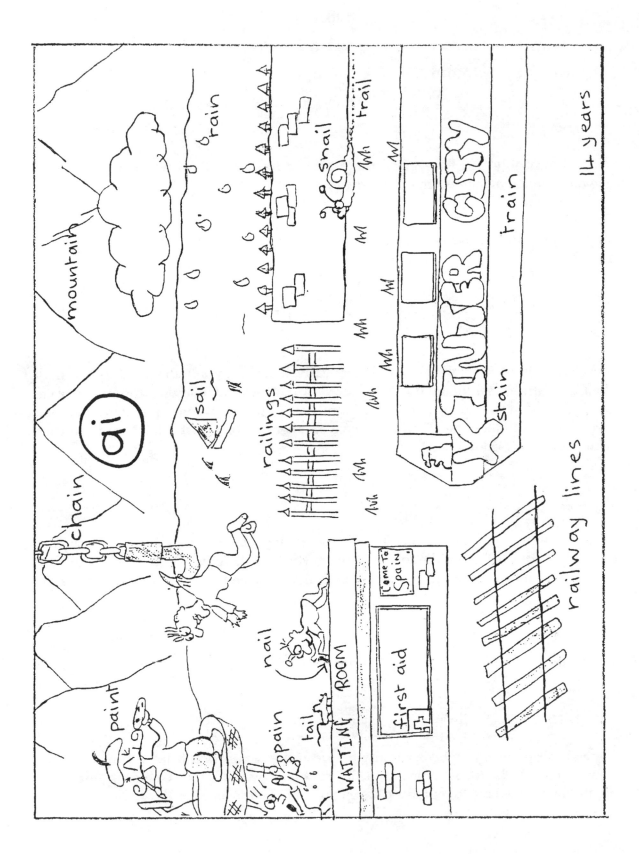

Revise some Blends

This is a good time to revise a few Blends. The words *rain*, *rail* and *nail* can be transformed by converting the first letter into various Blends, while *pain* and *wait* can be changed by using a Blend at the end.

rain		*rail*	*nail*	*pain*	*wait*
train	drain	trail	snail	paint	waist
brain	strain	frail			
grain	sprain				

Dictation sentences
The rain in Spain falls mainly on the plain.   Paint over the stain.
We will have to wait for the train in the rain.
Gail saw that the snail had left a trail from the drain.

-ay Box 6

I teach *-ay* next. In English we have no words that end in *i*. (*Ski* is Norwegian and *taxi* is short for taxicab.) If we want to miss off the final sound of *pain*, to make a different word, we can't write *pai*, because that ends in an *i*. Instead of the *i* we use a *y* and get the word *pay*. Therefore *-ay* is really a form of *ai*, which we use when the long $\bar{a}$ sound is the last part of a word. There are many words which use it.

day	may	away	decay	Sunday (etc.)
say	stay	stray	display	holiday
way	Kay	today	betray	yesterday
pay	Ray	delay	X-ray	birthday

Some *-ay* words can also be used for practising Blends.

ray		*way*	*lay*
tray	stray	sway	play
pray	spray		clay

Dictation sentences
Yesterday Ray got his holiday pay.   Kay will have an X-ray today.
You can play with the clay on the tray.   Stay for my birthday party on Sunday.

Chart 2   49

or and ore Box 12

The combination *or* is very common and it is often found in the middle of easy words.

for	cord	sort	north	doctor
fork	port	sport	report	record
form	horn	storm	corner	horse
torn	born	short	morning	inform
corn	pork	forget	story	platform
cork	York	forgive	history	ornament

Dictation sentences for or

Stick the fork into a cork.
His short story was about a horse.
The report said that she broke a sporting record.
Call the doctor in the morning and inform him that I fell off the platform.

There was a storm over the North Sea.
They have good pork in York.

As you will see from the list below, when we want to use *or* at the end of a word, we usually add an *e* and get the combination *ore*.

more	core	score	swore	before
sore (throat)	tore	snore	shore	explore
wore (a shirt)	bore	store	adore	ignore

When I enter *or* on my pupil's Chart 2, I write the *e*, which we sometimes need, in brackets.

Dictation sentences for or and ore

Just ignore her snores.
They must store more corn.
Come and explore the shore before you drink any more port.

He swore that he had a sore throat.
I adore her latest record.

er Box 11

This is often found at the ends of words.

her	ever	dinner	player	flower (plant)
term	never	supper	worker	September
after	every	letter	farmer	October
water	Mother	better	teacher	November

order	Father	litter	singer	December
anger	winter	butter	river	Peter
paper	summer	batter	shiver	Robert
silver	slipper	together	hover	Jennifer

The sound *er* is also used when we compare two things. For example,

That tree is *tall*, but this tree is *taller*.

Jim was *quick*, but Meg was *quicker*.

Dictation sentences
It is better if you put the litter in a bin.
The paper was never seen after that summer.
The singer, the farmer and the teacher all wanted to win the silver cup.
The diver will shiver when he gets out of the river.
Peter is a very good player. He hits every ball.

-alk Box 21

This is a very odd group of letters and it occurs in only four common words. So this is another very short list.

walk   talk   chalk   stalk (of a flower)

Dictation sentences
Will you walk and talk with me?   Hold the flower by the stalk.

oi- and -oy Box 14

I teach these together. It's a good way of reinforcing the rule of using *y* at the end of a word but *i* in the middle of a word. However, watch out, there are a few exceptions.

-oy		oi-		
boy	....	boil	boiler	avoid
joy	....	join	joint	joiner
toy	....	toil	toilet	voice
annoy		oil	spoil	spoilt
enjoy		coin	point	appoint

Chart 2   51

employ		coil	poison	appointment
destroy		soil	noise	disappoint
Roy		foil	choice	disappointment

Exceptions   royal   voyage   oyster

Dictation sentences

Avoid spilling the oil.
We will have to employ a joiner.

What sort of a noise annoys an oyster?
A noisy noise annoys an oyster.

ea Box 7

This makes exactly the same sound as *ee*. Your pupil may well be familiar with some 'sound-alike' words like *meat* and *meet*, or *weak* and *week*. Point out that many *ea* words are connected with food. I list them below in the first two columns.

eat	cream	seat	each	sea (water)
meat	wheat	east	teach	weak (not strong)
peas	cream	clean	reach	speak
beans	heat	cheap	ear	dream
peach	feast	cheat	hear	stream
tea	leaf	scream	fear	Jean

Dictation sentences

We will eat peas and beans with our meat.
Then we will each have a peach with cream.
I dream about sitting on a seat beside a clean stream, drinking weak tea.

Jean is a good teacher.
I fear that James is a cheat and a beast.

Sound-alikes

Spend a little time on the sound-alike words below.

meat .... meet

bean .... been

weak (not strong) .. week (7 days)

beach .... beech (tree)

read .... reed (plant)

beat .... beet (plant)

dear .... deer (animal)

sea .... see (eyes)

You can make up sentences to practise these sound-alikes. Ask the pupil to write out the sentences, choosing the correct word from each bracket.

Sam joined the navy to (sea see) the (sea see).

The red team (beat beet) the green team.

Have you (bean been) to the (beach beech) this (weak week)?

The letter *y* ... sometimes a consonant, sometimes a vowel

The letter *y* can make three sounds. When children are starting to learn to read and spell, *y* is taught as a consonant, in words like *yellow, yes, you* and *yo-yo*. In fact *y* is much more likely to be used as a vowel. We have already seen it 'taking the place of its best friend *i*', at the ends of words like *pay* and *boy*, because we can't use *i* at the end of a word. In these words it works with another vowel to make the *ay* and *oy* sounds. However, it also takes the place of *i* in other words, where it stands as a vowel on its own. Sometimes it makes a short ĭ sound; other times it makes a long ī sound.

y as a long vowel (ī) Box 8

This is often found in short words and children meet it when reading simple books. It crops up in longer words too.

my	fry	shy	apply	cycle
dry	sky	why	supply	satisfy
cry	spy	reply	occupy	multiply
fly	try	by (not shopping)		

Dictation sentences

The paint is dry.
My kite will fly in the sky.
He locked his cycle to the railings.

He did try to reply.
I will try to multiply.

y as a short vowel (ĭ) Box 27

The easiest way to show this is at the end of words like *lady, tidy, funny* and *penny*. Don't stretch the sound to say words like *funnee*. Remember short vowels have to be as short as possible. The short *ў* also occurs in more difficult words. The three last words in the lists below each have two short *ў*s.

baby	bully	story	factory	cylinder
lazy	silly	city	quantity	system
tiny	lolly	pity	quality	pyjamas
pony	sorry	handy	community	bicycle

Chart 2   53

cosy	foggy	sandy	history	capacity
happy	sunny	fifty	Tony	sympathy
messy	smelly	sixty	Wendy	symphony
jelly	jazzy	seventy	Mary	mystery

Did you notice that, although the *y* in *bicycle* is short, the *y* in cycle is long?

Dictation sentences

He is a lazy, dirty, smelly bully.
Tony is going to study the history of the army.
The old lady was happy in her tidy, cosy room.
Tony told a silly story about a man in funny pyjamas riding a tricycle.
The baby is messy when she has jelly or a lolly.
hen Wendy was twenty she was a cleaner at a factory.

To sum up the letter y

y – consonant	*y (ī) – vowel*	*y (ĭ) – vowel*
yes	sky	happy
yellow	dry	silly

kn- Box 16

Children seem to learn about this silent *k* very quickly although it doesn't occur very often. When I enter *kn* on the Chart, I write the *k* in pencil to emphasise that it is silent. I do the same for the other silent letters in this box.

knot (in string)	knob	knee	knock
knife	knit	kneel	knight (on horseback)

Dictation sentences

If I get a knot in my knitting I cut the wool with my knife.
Do not knock your knee on the knob.   The knight will kneel for the king.

Look-alikes

The letter combination *ow* can make two sounds. It can make the last sound in *snow* or the last sound in *cow*. Consequently *ow* appears in Box 15 as well as Box 9. The result of this is that we have some look-alike words. Good examples are *bow*, *row* and *sow*. It's impossible to know how to pronounce these words unless you know their context. For example:

He picked up his *bow* and arrows.   The gentleman must *bow*.

The girls stood in a *row*.   They had a blazing *row*.

The gardener will *sow* her seeds in Spring.   A mother pig is called a *sow*.

ow (snow) Box 9

In nearly all the words below, the *ow* comes at the end of the word.

low	crow	own	yellow	know (something)
below	grow	bowl	shadow	tomorrow
slow	blow	elbow	follow	narrow
show	throw	window	borrow	sparrow

Dictation sentences

I know the man is in the shed.   Follow the arrows.
I can see his shadow.   Tomorrow I will show you my yellow bowl.
I could see a crow and a sparrow in the snow below us.
I scraped my elbow getting out of the narrow window.

Combination words

In English we have words that are made by combining two small words. *Snowman* is a good example. *Snow* can be combined with several other words. See how many of these your pupil can think of. He may need some clues like, 'A flower', or 'You throw this'.

snowman	snowball	snowflake	snowstorm
snowmen	snowdrift	snowdrop	snowshoes

oa Box 9

This combination of letters seems to crop up in short words and it is another way to make the long ō sound. Once more the *name* of the first vowel gives the correct sound for the two vowels together.

boat	road	loaf	coach	throat
coat	load	oak	roast	goal
goat	toad	cloak	toast	soak
float	coal	soap	boast	Joan

Chart 2   55

Dictation sentences

We need another loaf to make toast.
Our coach was happy when we got lots of goals.
The stoat with a brown coat and a white throat ran down the road past the oak tree.

Look out for toads on the road.
The goat saw the boat float past.

-igh(t) Box 8

This goes into the *i-e* box and shouldn't really have the *t* at the end, but very few words use it without a *t*. The only common ones are **high**, **sigh** and **thigh**. A list of words with a *t* is below.

night	fight	bright	slight	delight
light	tight	fright	tonight	lightning
sight	might	flight	midnight	right (hand) (answer)

Dictation sentences

My right boot is tight.
The lightning gave me a fright.

Look at the bright light, high in the sky. What a sight!
The mighty knight will fight tonight.

Revision using parts of the body

Ask your pupil if he has a thigh and where it is. Does he have more than one? Many children don't know the word **thigh**. Get your pupil to draw himself and label all the parts of his body. He will probably need to draw a separate picture of his face because there will be so many labels for that. This activity is a good way to revise previous work. You can't expect to have every word spelt correctly, but you can see if he is using the sounds you have taught him. While he is doing this, his Chart 2 should be used to help him. If he is unsure about a spelling, try to guide him to the correct letter combination on the Chart, rather than just tell him what to write. He should be able to spell words like **leg**, **hip**, **hand** and **lip** very easily. In the list below I have underlined the letter combinations that have been taught so far.

chin	heel	nail	neck	finger
foot	nose	ear	arm	waist
back	face	teeth	toe	elbow

Of course the child will want to use awkward words like **eye** and **shoulder** that don't obey the phonic rules. Supply them as 'Look and Say' words.

This way of revising by choosing a topic, drawing a picture and labelling it, is a method that can be used over and over again. A motor bike or a car make good subjects. So does a house. Perhaps a picture illustrating a favourite story would appeal.

ir Box 11

This is much less common than *er*. Several *ir* words can be made into a picture like the one on page 58.

girl	shirt	third	dirty	first
sir	skirt	thirteen	thirsty	birth
bird	stir	thirty	birthday	circus
fir (tree)	firm	circle	confirm	Shirley

Dictation sentences

Thirty girls went to the circus.
Bring all the dirty shirts and skirts.

Shirley saw thirteen birds in the fir tree.
I went to his first birthday party.

ew Box 10

The first letter of this combination does not give any clue to its sound, but many children can write *new* and your pupil may be able to work out the sound of the letters *ew* from this word. The list below is not long but it contains some useful words.

new	chew	flew (fly)	drew (picture)
knew (something)	screw	grew (grow)	newspaper
few	crew	blew (blow)	Andrew
stew	jewel	threw (throw)	

Dictation sentences

We need a few new screws.
The crew threw the stew away.

The wind grew stronger and blew my hat off.
Andrew knew the jewels were kept in the bank.

Adding endings to words (2) Doubling Rule

Many people are confused about when they should double a letter. There is a very good rule about this. Suppose you were writing *fit* and wanted to add *-ing* would you double the *t* or not? You must ask *four questions*, one about the ending, and three about the word itself. Here we go.

First look at the ending.

Question 1.   Does it start with a vowel?   .....   YES.

Chart 2   57

*Next look at the root word **fit***.

Question 2.	Is it a short word?	(one clap)	.....	YES.
Question 3.	Has it a short vowel?	(ă, ĕ, ĭ, ŏ, ŭ)	.....	YES.
Question 4.	Is there only one consonant after the vowel?		.....	YES.

If you get four YES answers, you must double.

fit + ing = fitting

Take another example. We will use **fit** again. This time we will add **-ness**.

Question 1.	Does the ending start with a vowel?	.....	NO.

There is no need to ask any more questions.

fit + ness = fitness.

One more example. We will add **-ing** to **help**. Go through the four questions. You should get YES, YES, YES, NO for your answers. The **p** at the end of **help** will never double, no matter what ending you add to the word, because there are two consonants after the vowel.

Once the Doubling Rule is understood, there should be no confusion between the words, hopping ... hoping   filling ... filing   planning ... planing

The vowel *before* the double consonant is short. There's a simple sentence to help you remember this.

We had a super supper.

One more minor point, a little curiosity. We never double a *v*, even when the vowel before it is short. For example, *river, shiver* and *hover*.

Many people throw up their hands in horror and roll their eyes to heaven when I first explain this Doubling Rule. I tell them that once you practise it a few times, it's not all that difficult and, unlike some other rules, it has very, very few exceptions. I have never had a pupil who couldn't cope with it, and when a pupil is able to decide when to double a letter, it gives him quite a sense of achievement. It's surprising how many parents, sitting in on lessons, have said, 'I never knew when to double a letter. I'll remember that!'

Chart 2 is now partly completed

Perhaps this is a good time to pause and take a look at your Chart 2. Now that the Chart is filling up, check that your pupil is remembering the sounds of the letter combinations.

One activity that makes this a bit more interesting uses self-sticking, removable notes. These are small sheets that come in pads and have a sticky band across the top. They stick very well but can be peeled off easily. Take a sheet and cut off a strip, about 3 cm wide, that includes the sticky part and also some of the non-sticky part. This strip should then be cut across into little pieces about 0.5 cm wide.

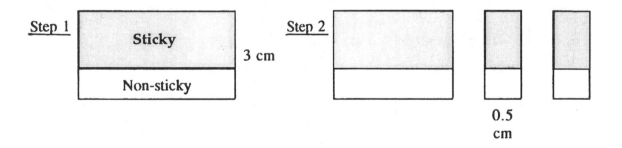

These little pieces (3 cm x 0.5 cm) will stick to your partly completed Chart and the non-sticky parts make them easy to pull off again. If a pupil can say a sound correctly, he can cover it. You will both soon see which sounds he is not sure about and need revising. Don't let him say all the sounds in one box straight after each other – that's too easy. He must keep going to different boxes. When you have finished your check, you can stick your little cover-ups on another page to use on another occasion. On page 60 you can see a partly completed Chart 2 with some of the sounds covered up.

Chart 2 59

PARTLY COMPLETED CHART 2

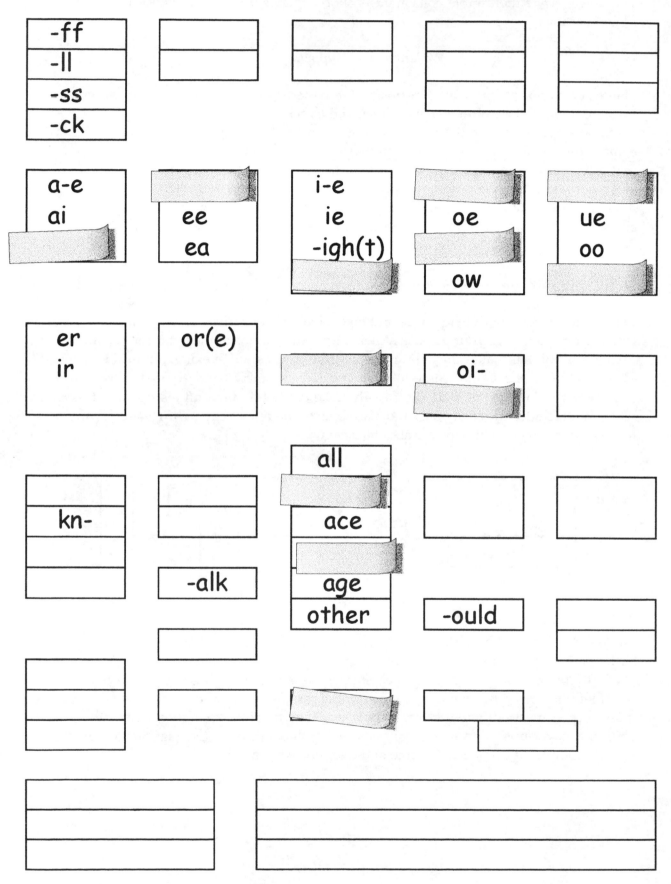

Teaching Reading and Spelling to Dyslexic Children

ce, ci and cy   Box 4

In these three groups of letters the *c* is soft. It makes the same sound as *s*. You can hear it in words like *dance, city* and *cycle*. People who read and spell easily have often never realised that *c* can make two different sounds and that there is a rule about it. Whenever *c* is followed by *e, i,* or *y,* it makes the same sound as *s*. In order to help pupils remember which vowels change and soften *c,* I write the vowels like this, adding *y,* which we know by now can swop places with *i*.

I deliberately squash the *e* and *y* to make them look thin. The big, fat, round ones *a, o* and *u* have no effect on *c*s but the 'thin' vowels soften the *c*. After you have talked about *c* sometimes saying *s,* you have to judge whether your child can cope with *ce, ci* and *cy* in one teaching session. If you are unsure, see how he manages *ce* words first.

ce   Box 4

The combination *ce* is very common and all the *ace* and *ice* words could be listed under *ce*. I give one example of each as a reminder. You can now point out that the *e* in these words is doing two jobs. It is lengthening the first vowel ($\bar{a}$ or $\bar{i}$) so that it says its name, and it is also softening the *c*.

cell (prison)	centre	prince	accept	concentrate
mice (etc.)	central	princess	succeed	centimetre
race (etc.)	distance	certain	century	excellent
dance	cement	Janice	except	certificate
chance	since	Alice	exercise	ceremony
fence	cancel	Vincent	advance	celebrate

Look at the two *c*s in *accept* and *succeed*. The first *c* is hard because it is followed by another *c,* but the second *c* is soft because it is followed by *e*.

Revision – syllables

Some words in the previous list are quite long, and so it is a good time to revise counting syllables, perhaps by clapping. Ask your pupil to write down a few of the longer words, chop them up into syllables and check that each syllable has at least one vowel.

Chart 2   61

prin/cess   cer/ti/fi/cate

ci Box 4

This combination is fairly common.

pencil	circle	cigarette	circulate	circumstance
acid	cinema	excited	incident	civilisation
cider	decide	circus	accident	Francis

Accident is like *accept,* in that it has one hard *c* and one soft *c*. This time it is because the second *c* is followed by *i*.

cy Box 4

This is not common in simple words.

cycle	tricycle	cyclone	Cyprus	Nancy
bicycle	fancy	anticyclone	cylinder	Lucy

Dictation sentences for soft c
Alice drew a circle with her pencil.
Vincent went to the city on his bicycle.

Nancy and Lucy decided to go to the cinema.
Janice had an accident at the fence.

ge, gi and gy   Box 5

Once the pupil has understood soft *c*s, tell him that there is one other letter that is softened. The good news is that it is softened by the same three vowels, *e, i* and *y*. This letter is *g*, and instead of making the hard sound we hear in *go*, it makes the same sound as *j*.

ge Box 5

Notice in the list below that *ge* is often found at the ends of words. This is because no English word ends in *j*. We use *ge* instead. Remind your pupils about the *age* words because they could be included in this list too.

gem	large	danger	college	intelligent

germ	charge	general	revenge	surgeon
German	ginger	hinge	geology	Angela
wage (etc.)	strange	gerbil	geography	George
huge	gentle	angel	emergency	Nigel

gi Box 5

This is not as common as *ge*.

gin	giant	gigantic	region	imagine
ginger	gipsy	engine	register	religion
magic	giraffe	engineer	regiment	Virginia

Did you notice that we can have *ginger* on two lists because it has two soft *g*s? Another point to notice – *gigantic* has one soft *g* and one hard *g*.

gy Box 5

There are only a few common words that use this combination.

gym	gypsy	energy	Egypt
allergy	geology	gymnasium	gymnastics

Did you notice that you can write *gipsy* or *gypsy*?

Dictation sentences for soft *g*.

George likes ginger cake.
Angela is in danger.
The intelligent surgeon went to college in Germany.
My gerbil got out of his cage and chewed a page of Nigel's geography book.

Imagine gigantic, magic giraffes in Egypt.
The general went to the gym.

Find the soft *c*s and *g*s

After teaching soft *c* and soft *g* your pupil will need practice in picking them out. In the list below some words have a soft *c*, some have a soft *g*, and some have neither. Copy some of the words and ask your child to underline the soft *c*s and *g*s. It's much easier to look for all the *c*s first, and then go through the list a second time looking for the *g*s.

generous	garage	prick	gipsy	golf	rage
stranger	cinema	cotton	caramel	centre	geography

Chart 2   63

caravan	icy	crash	grill	page	cash
dungeon	civilian	pencil	strangle	change	acre
candle	giraffe	crisps	angel	central	giant
general	mice	city	cylinder	celery	ceiling
price	glass	angle	rack	crab	gymnastics

-le Box 25

This is an extremely common ending. There are hundreds of words that end in -le. We occasionally use -el in words like *chapel*, *label*, *model* and *vowel*, but if your pupil is in any doubt about which one to use, tell him to go for -le. Often -le follows a double consonant and then, of course, the vowel before the double is short, as in these words,

saddle	nettle	scribble	bottle	struggle
battle	pebble	middle	wobble	cuddle

If there are two different consonants after the vowel, the vowel is short in these cases too.

candle	simple	single	grumble	handle
jumble	castle	strangle	bundle	ankle
gamble	scramble	mumble	stumble	gentle

If there is only one consonant before the -le, the vowel is long, as in these words.

title	bible	noble	bugle	table

Dictation sentences
The bible is on the table.   They found a single candle in the stable.
We took our bundle of jumble to the hall.
He landed in the middle of the nettles and broke his ankle.
In the battle for the castle he fell from his saddle.

-dge and -tch Box 2

This is the other box that I outline in red because these are also endings for short words with short vowels. They don't usually cause problems in reading, but spelling them can give trouble. This is because we don't pronounce the *d* in words like *hedge*, or the *t* in words like *ditch*. In fact I draw attention to these silent letters by writing the *d* and *t* in pencil when I enter the sounds on Chart 2.

-dge *Box 2*

Ed on the edge

This well known phrase, which I learnt from Gill Cotterell, is the best way I know of remembering about the silent *d* in this group of letters. My pupils always like to draw the picture of Ed on the cliff, at the bottom of the *-dge* word list in their hard-backed books.

badge	edge	bridge	lodge	judge
	hedge	fridge	dodge	smudge
	ledge	ridge		fudge
	wedge			grudge
	sledge			

Dictation sentences

Mrs Smith will judge the fudge at the show.   Put a wedge under the edge of the fridge.
The man hid on a ledge under the bridge.
Our sledge crashed into the hedge and I lost my badge.

-tch *Box 2*

When I teach this combination, I use the phrase 'The *cat catch*es ...' to help my pupil remember about the *t* which we don't hear. I let my pupil choose what it is that the cat catches, perhaps a ball or a bird, and once more he may like to illustrate this.

catch	fetch	itch	Scotch	hutch
patch	sketch	pitch		Dutch
match	stretch	ditch		crutch
snatch	witch			clutch
scratch	stitch			
thatch	switch			

There are a few well-known exceptions to the *-tch* rule. The words *such, much, rich* and *which* are short words with short vowels, but they don't have the silent *t*. I find it's best not to mention these because they don't normally give trouble, and it's pointless to give out unnecessary information.

Chart 2 65

Dictation sentences

I must scratch if I itch.
Strike a match or switch on the light.
The Dutchman will fetch his catch of fish.

Sketch a witch on her broomstick.
The pitch is marked out for the match.

ur Box 11

This is the last group of letters to go into Box 11. It is more common than *ir*, but nowhere near as common as *er*.

fur (cat)	church	return	surprise	furniture
hurt	purse	turtle	nursery	burglar
curl	nurse	Thursday	surgeon	disturb
turn	curse	Saturday	murder	urgent
burn	purple	turkey	murmur	Arthur

Dictation sentences

The nurse curled her hair to go to church.
Arthur will cook Xmas dinner and he will not burn the turkey.
I was surprised when it was returned on Saturday.

I lost my purple purse last Thursday.

ke- and ki- Box 3

I teach the rule about these two letter combinations by producing a set of words on small cards. The words I use are below. I also have seven cards with single letters, *a, e, i, o, u, l* and *r*. The single letters are spread across the table and the child is asked to put the words underneath them, according to the *second* letter of each word. The result should look something like this.

a	*e*	*i*	*o*	*u*	*l*	*r*
camp	keen	kite	cold	cut	class	creep
candle	keep	kid	cot	custard	click	crust
cave	kettle	kiss	cobweb	cup	close	cross
cap	Ken	king			clock	cress
		kipper			cloth	crash
		kill				
		kitten				

Ask the child which letters come in front of *e* and *i*. Can they work out why this is? Box 4 has something to do with it. Some children will be able to work out, all by themselves, why we use *ke-* and *ki-*, but others will need help. If we have a *c* in front of these two vowels it will make a soft *s* sound. Look back at the Soft *c* lists. The rule is if you want a *k* sound, use a *c* unless the next letter is *e* or *i*. A few more *ke-* and *ki-* words are given below.

key	kennel	kit	kind	kidnap
keeper	kestrel	kick	kilt	kidney

Dictation sentences
The king kicked the kettle.   We will kidnap the kid when we get the key.
Ken was keen to play football but he had left his kit at home.
Keep the dog in his kennel until we find the kitten.
The keeper of the kestrel was kind to the bird.

Plurals (2) Change **y** to **i** and add **es** ... but not always!

By this stage many children can write *baby* and *babies*, but often they have not really appreciated that the *y* has been changed to *i* (because it is no longer the last letter of the word) and then an *es* has been added, not just an *s*. There are many words like this.

lady ... ladies	jelly ... jellies	copy ... copies
pony ... ponies	lolly ... lollies	reply ... replies
cry ... cries	penny ... pennies	supply ... supplies
fly ... flies	bully ... bullies	injury ... injuries
spy ... spies	dolly ... dollies	burglary ... burglaries
body ... bodies	berry ... berries	galaxy ... galaxies

You will notice that all the words in the lists above have a consonant in front of the *y*. However, in some other words the *y* is connected to another vowel, as happens in the sound *ay* and *oy*, and in these words we don't change the *y*. All we do is add an *s*. Sometimes *y* is combined with *e* and these words just need an *s* too.

days	plays	boys	keys	kidneys
ways	trays	toys	monkeys	jockeys
says	delays	decoys	donkeys	turkeys
jays	holidays		valleys	chimneys

If your pupil has difficulty with the plurals in the dictation sentences below, ask him to write out the singular word first on scrap paper and take a good look at it to see if the *y*

Chart 2 67

stands alone, or if it works together with another vowel. If the *y* is working with another vowel, it's easy – just add *s*.

Dictation sentences
There were long delays before the ladies and the boys set off on their holidays.
The jockeys raced the donkeys and the ponies.
The monkeys, turkeys and jays all ate berries.
I sent sixty copies of the letter out and I have had only twenty-two replies.
The men in the valleys had many injuries and supplies were getting low.

ou Box 15

This group of letters is never used at the end of a word. If a word ends in this sound, we use *ow* (the next sound) instead. The *ou* combination is often used before *nt* and *nd* as you can see in the fourth and fifth columns below.

out	sour	house	count	found
about	proud	mouse	counter	round
our	cloud	flour (bread)	county	sound
hour	south	sprout	mount	ground
loud	mouth	trout	mountain	pound
aloud	shout	trousers	fountain	hound

Dictation sentences
We gave a loud shout and the mouse ran round the fountain.
Mum and Dad are proud of our new house.
In the south of the county the ground is flat.
There was cloud on the mountain for about three hours.

ow (cow) Box 15

As you can see from the first column below, *ow* is sometimes used to end a word.

how	owl	down	crown	power
now	howl	town	frown	shower
vow	growl	clown	towel	flower (plant)
allow	crowd	brown	vowel	tower

Dictation sentences

The old brown dog growled and howled.

After a shower you need a towel.

Now the owl nests in the old tower.

How did you get down town?

The clown has a crown of flowers.

wr- Box 16

When I enter this combination on the chart, I write the *w* in pencil because it is silent. There are not many words that have a silent *w*. Five of them are forms of the verb, *to write*. However, I find it helps to list them because they are used so much. Ask your pupil why *written* has two *t*s. (The rule for double consonants is explained on page 57.)

write	writer	wrote	wrist	wrinkle
writing	written	wrong	wrap	wriggle

Dictation sentences

She wrote the letter in her best handwriting.

I will wrap a bandage round your wrist.

Don't wriggle or it will wrinkle.

You have put it on the wrong wrist.

-air and *-are* Box 19

Children usually know the word *air* when they reach this stage, but they have to be warned that *-are*, which is only part of a word, does not make the same sound as the word *are*. The sound-alike *hair* and *hare* are usually enough to show them that *-air* and *-are* make the same sound.

air	hair	.... hare (animal)	care	beware
chair	fair	.... fare (bus)	spare	prepare
pair (2)	stairs	.... stare (eyes)	share	compare
repair	upstairs	bare (leg)	scare	declare
Clair	downstairs	dare	square	Clare

Dictation sentences

Can you repair my chair?

Prepare a pair of square patches.

Clair / Clare always takes care to share the money fairly.

We paid our fare and went upstairs in the bus to find two spare seats.

The hare is scared of the dog.

Clair / Clare has fair hair.

Chart 2 69

Adding pieces onto the beginnings of words (prefixes)

We have already looked at adding extra pieces onto the *ends* of words (suffixes, pages 40 and 57). We also add pieces onto the beginnings of words, and these are called prefixes. If you can recognise these extra pieces, it will improve your reading and spelling, as well as helping with the meanings of words. Some prefixes are so common that your pupil will have been using them already without any trouble. A good example is *un-* which changes a word to mean the opposite, as in *happy* and *unhappy*. However, other prefixes need to be taught. Many children make mistakes like *allways* and *alltogether* because they know that the word *all* has double *l*. They need to learn that when *all* is used as a prefix it has only one *l*. Here are a few useful *al-* words.

always   almost   already   also   although   altogether

It's very easy to find words using a particular prefix by using a dictionary, but be careful. If you look up words starting with *al*, for example, you will find that they are not all using the prefix *al-*. If you took the *al* off the word *altitude*, you would be left with *titude*, which is not a word. Remember that a prefix is an extra piece put onto the front of a *word*, not just in front of a group of letters.

There are a huge number of prefixes and it's easy to become too involved with them. I have listed a few of the most useful ones below, together with their meanings and some words that are made with them.

Prefix	Meaning	Examples
un-	not	untidy, unlucky, unable, unfit
in-	not	incomplete, indirect, inaccurate
re-	again	refill, recapture, rebuild, reconsider
pre-	before	preview, premature, prefix
mis-	badly	misfire, misbehave, misunderstand

Some words have prefixes and suffixes, and this often results in daunting, long words. *Disappointment* is one example. It has fourteen letters, but, if you recognise the bits which have been added and cover up *dis* and *ment*, you are left with the much simpler seven-letter word *appoint*. It's easy to uncover the other pieces and read the whole word. This habit of thinking about a long word in sensible chunks helps both spelling and reading.

-mb Box 16

There are not many common words that end in this curious way. These are the most useful.

lamb   limb   numb   dumb   climb

bomb   thumb   crumb   comb

Dad had to climb into the attic.   He hit his thumb and made it numb.
My pet lamb will not eat crumbs.   She lost a limb as a result of a bomb.

-tion Box 25

This is a very peculiar group of letters. The *ti* makes the same sound as *sh*. The fact that it is such a strange group of letters seems to appeal to children, and helps them to remember it. The words in the following word list look horrific, but believe me they are not. Start with easy ones like *mention* and *condition*. They probably know the word *station*. Get the pupil to clap the syllables and write the words in these chunks, *men-tion* and *con-di-tion*. When you break these long words into syllables, your pupil will probably find that they are much easier than he thought. Don't forget to praise your pupil's efforts. You are now reading and spelling some difficult words. Later on, when your pupil is confident with *-tion*, you may be able to tackle more endings using *ti* to make the *sh* sound. There are examples in Appendix 5.

station	direction	election	relation	examination
nation	infection	opposition	education	decoration
action	addition	revolution	dictation	population
mention	subtraction	inspection	operation	generation
fiction	solution	affection	information	explanation
fraction	attention	protection	conversation	determination
condition	promotion	ammunition	imagination	civilisation

Dictation sentences
The opposition hopes to win the election.   Use your imagination and think of a solution.
Please will you give me directions to the station?
She paid attention to her work and soon got promotion.
What action can we take to give our wild flowers protection?
After the operation he had an infection, in addition to his weak condition.

au Box 12

Like *ou*, this combination does not occur at the end of a word. In both cases we use a *w* instead of the *u* if the sound is the last part of the word. The lists for *ow* and *aw* come later.

cause	haunt	August	exhaust	Austria
because	pause	autumn	automatic	Australia

Chart 2 71

sauce	author	caution	autograph	Paul
fault	audience	auction	dinosaur	Laura

Dictation sentences

Laura paused by the haunted house.   Paul is going to Austria in the autumn.

In August we sent the old automatic washer to the auction rooms.

There was a pause before the audience started applauding.

It was not my fault that the sauce was spoiled.

How some of our longest words are made

This is a good point to have a break from teaching letter combinations and the sounds that they make. We have now come across some very long words and we have seen how prefixes and suffixes can be dropped off, to simplify reading or spelling a word, and then put back on. We can take big words to pieces in another way. Two of the words in the previous group start with *auto*. This means *self*. An *automatic* machine controls itself. Of course we have to start an automatic washing machine, but we don't have to decide when it should drain, spin or rinse. It organises these operations without us. Take another example, *autograph*. The last part *-graph* means writing or drawing, so your *autograph* is your own name written by yourself. *Biology* is an interesting word. *Bio* means *life*, and *-logy* means *study*, therefore *biology* is the study of living things – plants and animals. We can combine bits of the words *autograph* and *biology* to make *biography*, a piece of writing about someone's life. If we take apart that lovely word, *autobiography*, auto-bio-graphy we get *self, life, writing* – someone writing about their own life. Some people find taking big words to pieces is fascinating, but it doesn't appeal to everyone. I suggest you try it out and see what reaction you get. Although I believe that it helps with spelling and knowing the meanings of words, don't pursue it if the feedback is not favourable. If you want another group of words to take to pieces, try *telephone, television, telescope, telepathy* and *telecommunications*. Your pupil may be able to work out what they all have in common. It's *distance*.

aw Box 12

These letters make the same sound as *or* and *au*. However, unlike *au*, the *aw* can be used at the end of a word.

saw	jaw	straw	crawl	lawyer
law	claw	lawn	hawk	awful
paw (dog)	draw	yawn	withdraw	awkward
raw (food)	thaw	prawn	outlaw	Dawn

Dictation sentences

Dawn thinks prawns are awful.

I saw something crawl under the straw.

Cats can draw their claws back into their paws.

Cutting the lawn makes me yawn.

Dogs have strong jaws and can eat raw meat.

Plurals (3) Change *f* to *v* and add *(e)s*

Your pupil probably knows some of these plurals, but it is worth making a list, in order to draw attention to the rule about changing *f* to *v*. Sometimes we don't need to add an *e* before the *s*, because the singular word already has one.

wife	....	wives	loaf	....	loaves	thief	....	thieves
life	....	lives	half	....	halves	wolf	....	wolves
knife	....	knives	calf	....	calves	shelf	....	shelves
leaf	....	leaves					

Dictation sentences

Cut all the loaves into halves.

The wives have happy lives.

They killed the wolves with their knives.

The thieves took everything off the shelves.

The calves will not eat those leaves.

ph Box 24

I introduce this box by talking about where some of our words come from. Words that use *ph* instead of *f* usually started off as Greek words. How did they get into our language? This is the simplified, but perhaps not completely accurate, story that I tell.

About 500 years before Christ was born, the Greeks were the most advanced people in Europe. However, by the time of Christ, the Romans had gained control over the Greeks and they had taken many Greek words into their language, which was Latin. The Romans had a huge empire and Latin influenced the languages of many of the countries they ruled. One of these countries was France and the French language is largely based on Latin. When William the Conqueror sailed from northern France in 1066, and made himself king of England, he and his victorious knights settled in England but spoke French. Gradually the languages merged and French words that had previously come from Latin, and before that from Greek, were now part of English.

I have selected a few words that show how the Greek *ph* has persisted into modern English.

Greek ⟶	Latin ⟶	French ⟶	English
elephas	elephantus	éléphant	elephant
sphaira	sphera	sphère	sphere
alphabetos	alphabetum	alphabet	alphabet

Chart 2   73

Not all our *ph* words came from the Ancient Greeks. They didn't have *photographs* or *telephones*, for instance. These words were concocted because these inventions had to be called something, and often people went back to Greek and Latin for inspiration. When a name was needed for an invention that brought pictures to us from far away, *tele* (distance) was taken from Greek and *vision* (pictures) from Latin. So although some of our *ph* words are modern, their roots are in ancient languages. If you are interested in where words come from, a good dictionary will be a constant source of pleasure. More *ph* words are listed below.

photo	photograph	geography	trophy	Philip
phone	telephone	physics	orphan	Joseph
graph	paragraph	physical	emphasise	Stephen
dolphin	nephew	atmosphere	phantom	Daphne
phrase	triumph	microphone	sphinx	Ralph

Dictation sentences

Joseph telephoned about the dolphins.   I want to take a photograph of the sphinx. Stephen said that his nephew, Philip, was good at physics and geography.

ch (k) Box 24

I often teach this sound straight after *ph* because all the rigmarole about *ph* words applies to English words that use *ch* to make the same sound as *k*. Many of them came from Greek. Here are three examples.

Greek	→	Latin	→	French	→	English
skhole		schola		école		school
ekho		......		écho		echo
ankura		ancora		ancre		anchor

When my pupil is trying to read an unknown word, I tell him to try the more common sound of *ch* as in *chip* first. Then if that doesn't work try the *k* sound.

Christ	ache	chaos	mechanic	Christine
Christmas	chorus	stomach	technical	Christopher
Christian	orchestra	chemistry	technology	orchid
chemist	character	architect	scheme	Nicholas

Lots of adults don't know how to spell *chrysanthemum*. Now that your pupil has learnt about *ch* making a *k* sound, and also that *y* can do the same job as *i*, it's an easy word!

Chrys – an – the – mum. My pupils always like to spell this word to impress Mum and Dad.

Dictation sentences

Nicholas is a good mechanic.   We gave Mum a pot of chrysanthemums.

The chemist gave Christine something for her stomach ache.

The chorus and orchestra performed very well at Christmas.

The most important character in the story is an architect called Christopher.

-ind and *-ild* Box 17

I have included these on Chart 2 because, surprisingly, they both have a long *ī*.

-ind			*-ild*
kind	bind	blind	child
find	rind	grind	wild
mind	wind	behind	mild

Wind is another look-alike word.

> *Wind* up the string.   There is a strong *wind*.   The road *winds* round the hill.

Dictation Sentences

The nurse will be kind to the blind child.

You will find the grinder behind the large jug.

Mind your fingers when you grate the rind of the lemon.

What a bind! We will have to wind the wool again.

The wild flowers were beautiful and the weather was mild.

ea (*ĕ*) Box 26

If you ask your pupil to make the sound of *ea*, I hope he will say *ē*, as in *tea*. This is nearly always the correct sound for these letters. However, there are quite a few common words with *ea* which have a short *ĕ*.

head	thread	heavy	weather	heaven
bread	ahead	ready	feather	meadow
dead	instead	already	leather	pleasant
death	breath	spread	heather	pheasant
deaf	health	weapon	steady	breakfast

Chart 2 75

Silly Dictation

It was pleasant weather. The deaf peasant, dressed in leather, saw a pheasant drop a feather in the heather. With his weapon held steady, he shot it in the breast and head. It fell into the meadow, dead. When it was ready, he ate it with bread instead of potatoes because he dreaded scraping potatoes.

The fact that *ea* can be pronounced as a short *ĕ* or a long *ē*, means that we have at least two more look-alikes, *read* and *lead*.

gu Box 16

The *u* in this combination is silent, but it does a very important job. It acts as a barrier to keep the *g* away from *e* or *i*. Think about the words below. If the *u* was not there, the *g* would be softened into a *j* sound. (See page 62.)

guess	plague	league	intrigue	guide
guest	rogue	catalogue	fatigue	guilty
	vague	dialogue	synagogue	guitar
				disguise

Dictation sentences

We had a plague of ants.
The guide was a rogue.
The guilty man took off his disguise.

Our team plays in the local league.
Look at the guitars in the catalogue.
I had only a vague idea so I had to guess.

-ture Box 25

If you think your pupil can spell *picture*, ask him to write it down and work out what sound the ending *-ture* makes. He should pronounce it *cher*. He may then be able to write some of the easier words on the list below.

mixture	future	fracture	moisture	manufacture
fixture	lecture	structure	agriculture	architecture
capture	puncture	adventure	furniture	literature
nature	feature	creature	signature	temperature

Dictation sentences

We must capture the creature.
Let Norman shift the furniture in future.
The moisture disappeared when the temperature rose.

The lecture was about architecture.
Nature and agriculture exist side by side.

aught and ought Box 20

There are only a few common words that use these letter combinations. Fortunately the words that use *aught* are all included in this silly sentence:

I c*aught* my n*aught*y d*aught*er killing spiders and t*aught* her not to sl*aught*er them.

There are five useful words that contain *ought* to make the same sound. They are:

bought   fought   nought   brought   thought

ough Box 22

This group of letters is extremely awkward. If you ask me to make the sound of this letter combination, I wouldn't be able to give you a simple answer. It makes many different sounds, and so, until you see it in a word, you can't know what sound it makes. I put five red question marks around *ough* in Box 22 because it makes five different sounds in some common words. In the lists below I have shown the *sounds* in brackets above the words.

(ō)	(oo)	(ou)	(off)	(uff)
dough	through	plough	cough	rough
though		drought	trough	tough
although				enough

Dictation sentences
We have had enough of this drought.   The sea was rough but the crew was tough.
The pigs ran through the gate to their feeding trough.
Although he had a bad cough the farmer had to plough the next day.

wa and wo Box 28

You will notice that Box 28 is an odd shape. This is because something very strange happens when we have *wa* and *wo*. Pupils usually already know words that use these combinations. See if your pupil can spell *was, want, wasp, wash* and *watch*. When you have checked his spelling, see if he can work out what sound the *wa* is making. Yes, it's making the sound of *wo*. Very strange!

Now the question arises, what is happening in the words *won, wolf* and *woman*? You will find that the *wo* is making the sound of *wu*. When you understand the sounds that *wa* and *wo* make, there should be no confusion between *wander* and *wonder*.

If your pupil can already cope with all these words, don't labour the point. Simply congratulate him on learning them before he had the rule pointed out. If, on the other hand, you think that your pupil is going to find Box 28 difficult, take things very slowly and be sure to give him lots of praise for the effort that he makes.

Chart 2 77

Dictation sentences

I want you to have a wonderful day.

The woman saw a wolf wandering over the ice.

Walter won a watch.

Was that a wasp on the washing?

Revision – Clueless crosswords

Some children who hate doing normal crosswords will happily make what I call **Clueless Crosswords**, and they are very useful for revision. There are two kinds and you can see examples on page 79. The first one started with the word AUTOBIOGRAPHY written in the middle of a sheet of squared paper. The boy had to fill as many squares as he could, forming a crossword. When he had finished we counted the number of squares he had filled to get his score. On this occasion he scored 131.

I use Scrabble tiles for the second type of **Clueless Crossword**, but if you don't have these you can use your letter cards. Select 13 tiles at random and separate the vowels from the consonants. The challenge is to make a crossword using all your tiles. If you have a lot of vowels, you will have to combine them, and this means that you will be using the letter combinations on Chart 2. If you have only a few vowels, you will find that using Blends helps. Any tiles that are left over must be scored according to the little numbers on the tiles, and a really good result gives you a score of zero. When this happens, or else the score is very low, my pupils like to copy their crosswords into their exercise book.

Conclusion

If you have read this far, I am sure that you will appreciate the amount of effort Chart 2 calls for. Nobody finds it plain sailing. However I hope that you have managed to convince your pupil that, although English is not an easy language for spelling and reading, there *are* patterns and rules that can help. The routine of grouping letter combinations into their boxes, making short word lists, and using a Contents page, will also have given the child a framework for improving his spelling and reading. By now your pupil should feel confident about using his hard-backed book and be able to quickly look up any letter combination you have covered.

As well as being able to pick out common letter combinations and know the sound they represent, your pupil should now know:

- the difference between long and short vowels;
- how *y* can sometimes be a consonant and sometimes a vowel;
- how to break up words into syllables and that each syllable has at least one vowel;
- several prefixes and suffixes, and be able to add them to, and take them off, words;
- when to drop the final *e*;
- when to double the last letter of a word;
- which words need *es* when making them plural;
- which words need *f* changing to *v* when making them plural;
- when *c*s and *g*s become soft;
- how to find ways of helping himself to remember important things, with silly sentences or pictures etc.

CLUELESS CROSSWORDS

Type 1 starts with one big word:

	R	E	A	L	I	Z	E			B	A	S	H		D	
		A			O					H	A		B	O	A	T
		T		S	O	S				A	S	H		A		O
	S		C	A	P			T	E	A		E		T	A	P
	T				O			A		H				T		O
	A		A	U	T	O	B	I	O	G	R	A	P	H	Y	
	C	A	N							A	P		E		D	
	K		D	A	N	C	E			M	P		L			
			H	I		B	E	E		Y		L	O	G		
		P		C	A	T						O		O	N	
F	R	A	N	C	E		A	L	L		C		H	T	O	P
A	N	O	P				L	A		A		A			O	A
T	A	G	P			L	A	B	O	R	A	T	O	R	Y	T

Type 2 starts with 13 letters:

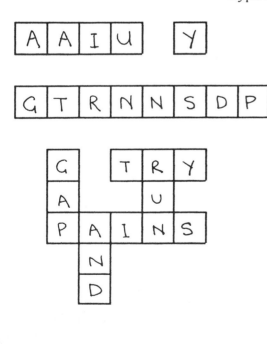

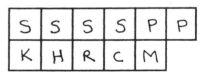

Chart 2 79

In future, any *regular* word that persistently gives him trouble can be entered in his hard-backed book. It will either start off a new word list and fill in another box, which will have been added, or it will go in a word list he already has, and consequently be linked with easier words which he already knows.

On the other hand, if he has a problem with an *irregular* word, he can enter it into his small indexed book of awkward words, which I mentioned on page 12.

As I said in my Introduction to Chart 2, there is no reason why you and your pupil shouldn't have a break from fairly concentrated efforts to improve his reading and spelling, but try not to let everything he has learnt slip away. The easiest way to do this is to arrange some times when you can continue to help him with his reading. After all, this is the most enjoyable part of the whole business. And speaking of enjoyment, try to keep a happy relationship with your pupil. When the going gets tough, simple crosswords or word puzzles can bring relief and enjoyment for both of you.

Punctuation

We don't need to worry about punctuation when we speak. It happens automatically. However, punctuation is very important when we write. It shows us how to say the words we read, and the way we say the words alters their meaning remarkably. Remember the old song, 'It ain't what you say, it's the way that you say it'.

> He was wrong. – just a flat statement.
>
> He was wrong? – a question. Was he really wrong?
>
> He was wrong! – could be said in anger or triumphantly, but certainly emphatically.

Full stop, question mark and exclamation mark

A sentence is a complete and sensible group of words, and we nearly always mark its end by using a full stop. But there are occasions when we use a question mark or an exclamation mark instead, as you can see from the sentences above. You can think of question marks and exclamation marks as different types of full stops. After all, they both include a dot, don't they? All three marks give the reader a chance to pause and take a breath.

Comma

We use a comma whenever we want the reader to pause only slightly, not as much as when he comes to a full stop. The two commonest uses of the comma are:

- when we are giving a list,
- to separate a phrase from the main part of a sentence. The sentence must still make sense without the phrase.

Here are examples. Notice, in the first sentence, that we use *and* instead of a comma between the last two items. In the second sentence, the phrase that could be taken out of the sentence is emphasised.

> We took sandwiches, cakes, fruit and biscuits.
>
> We ran on, *without looking back*, until we were safely on the main road.

Apostrophe

An apostrophe looks like a comma, but it's written higher up. You can see an apostrophe and a comma in my previous sentence. We use apostrophes to do two jobs.

1. to show when something *belongs*: the girl's bike, the car's brakes
2. to show that letters have been missed out in shortened words.
   was not ... wasn't   should not ... shouldn't   have not ... haven't

Notice also that the space between the words disappears when we shorten two words.

Ask your pupil to try shortening the words below. If he finds it difficult, it will help if he puts them into a sentence first, like this. *She will be late* changes to *She'll be late.*

she will	you are	do not	would not	they have
who have	it will	they are	she has	who will
could not	we are	he has	I will	he will
she is	we will	will not (won't)		

When your pupil can do this give him the shortened form of the words and see if he can change them back to the full version.

it's and *its*

Many people have no idea when *its* needs an apostrophe. It's quite simple really.

$$it's = it\ is \qquad or \qquad it's = it\ has$$

You need an apostrophe if you can say either *it is* or *it has*, instead of *its*. Here are some examples.

It's not fair!	*It is* not fair.
It's no good going that way.	*It is* no good going that way.
It's been late three times.	*It has* been late three times.
It's always been a holiday.	*It has* always been a holiday.

The following examples don't need an apostrophe. They don't make sense if you try to say *it is* or *it has*, instead of *its*.

The dog has lost its collar.	Its tyres are fairly new.
Each cow knows its own stall.	The cat often chases its tail.

Quotation marks (speech marks) (66–99) (inverted commas)

You can see that there are at least three other names for quotation marks. These marks enclose the actual words spoken. Some people prefer to use double marks, others prefer single ones. Double quotation marks are often used in handwriting and single quotation marks are usually used in books.

One way of teaching children when to use quotation marks is to start with a little cartoon, showing a character with a speech balloon. Then you rub out most of the circle that surrounds the words, until you are left with curved marks, a bit like quotation marks.

However, when your writing includes speech, you have to do more than put in the quotation marks. There are three things to remember altogether.

- Begin the first word of a speech with a capital letter.
- Use quotation marks to enclose the speech.
- Separate the speech from the rest of the sentence with a comma (unless you have just used a question mark or an exclamation mark). You can see examples of this in the punctuated story in the Answers section on page 103.

Here is a sentence that includes speech. It could be turned round.

'We went to the beach and it was lovely', said Carol.

Carol said, 'We went to the beach and it was lovely'.

It's not uncommon to have a split speech. If the *said Carol* comes in the middle of a sentence, you need an extra comma to separate it from the rest of the speech. Notice that we don't use a capital letter for the second part of a split speech.

'We went to the beach', said Carol, 'and it was lovely'.

Never use quotation marks unless you are writing the *exact* words that someone says. For example, *David said that his father was late*, does not need quotation marks because David didn't say the words, *'That his father was late'*.

One more point, if you are including speech in a story, each speech should start on a new line and be set in from the left side. If you look at any novel you will see this.

There are other times when we use quotation marks. Most people use them when handwriting titles of books although these can be underlined instead. Printed books normally use italics for book titles. We also use quotation marks when we include someone else's words in our writing, as older children sometimes do in their English essays. The example below is from Frances Hodgson Burnett's, *The Secret Garden*, and the words inside the quotation marks are taken from the book.

Mary's mother 'cared only for parties and smart people'.

Don't always use 'said'

Children use the word *said* far too much, and it makes their writing boring. Suggest one or two alternatives, such as, *shouted, asked, replied* or *explained,* and then look through a few pages of a book and see if you can find others. You could make a list of the most useful ones.

Colon and semicolon

Parents sometimes ask me about colons and semicolons, saying that they don't understand them. My advice is 'Forget about them. You can get along without them very nicely.' If your child can use the other punctuation marks properly he is doing very well.

Two punctuation exercises

In order to show how important punctuation is, I would like you to copy the following passage, putting in capital letters and full stops where necessary.

bob closed the door quietly he gave his orders in a few minutes the men crossed the car park being careful to move secretly next morning bob went to see joe in the room near the canteen there was a group of men talking excitedly

I hope you will find that you can punctuate this passage in different ways. For example, where does the word *quietly* belong, at the end of the first sentence or at the beginning of the second one? Was Joe in the room next to the canteen or not? Decide what you think is happening and use punctuation to convey your ideas. I have given just two possible versions on page 101, but there are others.

I have also written the following story without any punctuation. See what you make of it! I think you'll find it difficult to understand in this state.

on a hot monday in june rose mark and miles drove up to the tees on cross fell for a picnic they had been planning for some time they took cans of coca-cola chocolate biscuits an orange cake sandwiches and three apples is it far asked mark who didnt know that part of england good heavens no laughed miles well be there very soon in ten minutes they had parked the car unloaded their things and were enjoying their lunch among the buttercups they saw lots of white butterflies and two wasps came to sample the jam in the cake when they had finished eating they walked by the river all of a sudden rose yelled she had slipped and twisted her ankle miles looked at mark what shall we do shell never manage to walk back now well have to help her replied mark one on each side to give her support the strap on roses shoe had broken to add to their trouble it had started to rain and they were all soaked when they reached the car were not having a very good time are we moaned rose but the others said cheerily theyd had a good time until her accident she thought its all very well for you two well soon be home continued miles and when your ankle is attended to and weve all changed into dry clothes we can put up our feet and watch the telly for the rest of the journey home rose was very quiet she wished shed worn more sensible shoes

You can see a punctuated version of this story on page 103.

Spelling

Dictionaries

Dictionaries are especially useful to people who have trouble with spelling but, unfortunately, these are the very people who find them difficult and frustrating to use. Your pupil may be very reluctant to reach for a dictionary but it is important to change this attitude.

I usually introduce dictionary work by asking some questions like, 'How do you feel about using a dictionary?' 'Do you use one often and find it useful?' 'Perhaps you hate dictionaries and avoid them?' I also ask, 'What is a dictionary?' 'What do we use it for?' Children hardly ever say that dictionaries tell us what words mean. They usually answer, 'It's got lists of words in it', and, 'You can find out how to spell words'. This last answer lets you point out that if they had a dictionary that they could use easily, it would be really valuable. Besides, later on, we are going to have some fun with dictionaries!

We start by considering my collection of dictionaries. I have five, ranging from *My First Picture Dictionary* to the fat, heavy *Collins Dictionary of the English Language*. I ask my pupil to arrange them in some sort of order. Which one does he fancy? He usually settles for the middle of the range. My simplest dictionary has 5,000 words (*The Illustrated Oxford Dictionary*) and I have another with almost 20,000 words (*The Oxford Children's Dictionary*). If he is not sure which of these to go for, I encourage him to start with one with fewer words, because he will find the word he needs much quicker. If, later on, he finds that this dictionary hasn't got all the words he needs, he can move on to another with more words.

We spend some time talking about all the dictionaries. In what ways are they all the same? In what ways are they different? They all list words alphabetically and give meanings. My 5,000 word dictionary has the alphabet printed at the top of every page – extremely useful. It has pictures and each word is set out into the margin and printed in colour. If a word has more than one meaning, each meaning is clearly numbered, and sometimes phrases or short sentences show how we use that word in a particular way. For example, it gives four meanings for *point*.

My 20,000 word dictionary generally looks similar and also has an alphabet on each page, but there are fewer pictures. However, one very important advantage is that it gives various forms of words. For example, *luck* is followed by *lucky* and *luckily*, a useful reminder about changing the *y*. It also gives more meanings, nine for *point*, and tells you whether the word is a noun or a verb etc.

My next dictionary is a 'school' dictionary printed in 1951. How things have changed! It's not at all reader-friendly, but it gives information about the type of word (noun, verb, adjective) and some help about pronunciation. The reason that I show this book at all, is because this is the sort of dictionary that some children are expected to use. Even worse than this is a pocket dictionary with small print, and which also refuses to stay open.

Last of all is my Collins dictionary, a wonderful book to have on the shelf. It gives all the information I could reasonably want, and my pupils enjoy getting it out when we want to find out how words are related and which language they have come from. By the way, it gives fifty-five meanings for *point*.

I think it's worth while spending time comparing dictionaries. I always lend my pupils whichever dictionary they choose, so that they have a chance to get used to it. Then, if they go off with their Mum or Dad to buy their own dictionary, which I hope they will, they will know what features to look out for.

One reason why children dislike using a dictionary is that it takes them ages to find a word. They usually go down page after page, reading every word until they come to the word they are looking for. I discourage this by asking my pupil why he thinks there is a word at the very top of each of the two pages that he can see. It saves a lot of time when he realises that all the words on those two pages lie between the two words printed at the top.

Many people have great trouble remembering the order of the alphabet. If my pupil uses a dictionary that does not have the alphabet on each page, I make a bookmark for him to keep in his dictionary. The top of it looks like this *on both sides*.

A B C D E F G H I J K L M

N O P Q R S T U V W X Y Z

Wherever the pupil opens his dictionary the alphabet is visible, peeping out above the pages. Make sure the second line of letters starts with N to draw attention to the fact that M and N come in the middle of the alphabet.

Check that your child understands the alphabetical arrangement of the words. He may not realise that, when we have taken account of the first letter of a word, we look at its second letter, then the third letter and so on. If you write a few words on slips of paper and ask him to sort them alphabetically, you will soon see if he understands the system. Some of the words below are sorted by their second letter, others by their third, fourth or even fifth.

grape   glue   game   gasp   graph   gash

Looking at the bookmark I have described above, you may think that the first quarter of a dictionary would have words starting with A, B, C, D, E, F, and perhaps G. You would be wrong. If you look at a dictionary you will see that you have only reached the letter D when you are a quarter of the way through the book. This is because we have lots of words beginning with A, B, C and D, while very few of our words start with other letters like X, Y and Z. So it's no good looking in the first quarter of the book unless your word starts with A, B, C, or D. Believe it or not, this knowledge saves a lot of time. If you feel inclined, you can work out the other quarters of your dictionary. It will probably work out like this:

A B C D

E F G H I J K L

M N O P Q R

S T U V W X Y Z

I don't stress this too much, but your pupil may like these groups written in the front of his dictionary. I find that the most useful facts are that M and N are the middle two letters, and that the first quarter only covers the first four letters.

We are now ready to have our first bit of fun. It's a simple game where one person says a letter and the other person tries to open the dictionary at a page of words beginning with that letter. If he gets it right, he scores two points. If he gets a letter next to the one he is trying for, he gets one point. This quick, easy game will improve his speed when looking up a word.

The next game is my favourite dictionary game. The first player opens the dictionary and chooses a word, let's say *puppet*. He tells the other player the first letter of the word, *p*, and reads out the definition, 'A doll that can be made to move by wires or strings'. The second player has to guess the word. If he succeeds, he can choose the next word. If he doesn't get the correct word, the first player has another turn. Sometimes players give each other extra clues.

This game is useful for many reasons. First it gets a reluctant pupil to actually pick up and open a dictionary. This is a major step for some children. Next the child has some reading practice when he chooses a suitable word, and reads out the definition. If he has to give an extra clue, he will have to think about explaining the meaning of the word and express his ideas clearly. The game also enlarges his vocabulary. All this means that a child is practising a number of skills, while having fun solving puzzles.

Checking spellings without a dictionary

There are three things I have found useful when the *spelling* of a word is all that needs to be checked. The first is a book, the other two are electronic spellcheckers.

The book is called *Spell it yourself*, and generally gives no meanings. It is only for checking spellings. It's like a dictionary, but much easier to use. If I wanted to check the word *office*, I would go straight to the index at the back of the book. This lists only the first two letters of words, and I would see that words beginning with *of* are on page 63. Now I can go to the correct page immediately, and it's comparatively easy to find *office*. No turning page after page, and wondering if O comes before or after L. If there is another word which sounds exactly like your word, for example *groan* and *grown*, brief meanings are given, (moan; got bigger), so that you can be sure that you use the right one.

Besides giving you the basic word, *Spell it yourself* shows endings you can add. For example, *bake* can be changed to *baked*, *baking* (the symbol ¢ reminds us to drop the *e*), *baker*, *bakehouse* and *bakes*.

Electronic spellcheckers

Electronic spellcheckers fall into two groups, pocket and desk-top models, which are very easy to carry around, and those that are part of a word-processor on a computer.

Pocket and desk-top models vary a great deal. Some are very good, others are dreadful. Some have American spelling, or a screen that is too small for long words to fit on, and some are just too complicated.

Some people want a spellchecker that is easy to slip into a pocket or bag and is as inconspicuous as possible. For these people a pocket model is the answer.

For my teaching purposes I find a desk-top spellchecker much more satisfactory because the buttons are less fiddly and the screen is easier to read. The desk-top versions are usually a bit more expensive but prices vary considerably.

Many people who buy a spellchecker soon become frustrated and abandon it. One cause of despair is that the word lists are far too long. The result is that you find yourself scrolling down masses of words (some of which you've never heard of, let alone know what they mean!) desperately trying to find the one you want. This is a clear case of, 'More is certainly not better'.

Franklin make a range of electronic spellcheckers and the one I generally recommend is their Elementary Spellmaster, which comes with clear instructions and is suitable for a child who can read as well as an average seven year old. This model is not among the cheapest, but it has been designed with dyslexics in mind, and is very clever at recognising misspelt words which look very weird, as long as they have been typed in phonically, according to the sound of the word. I entered *geraf, jeraf, jiraf* and *jurafe*, and each time it came up with *giraffe*, which was what I wanted. If you type in *nolig*, it will offer *knowledge*, so you can see that it really tries hard to accommodate bizarre spelling.

The Franklin Spellmaster is linked to *The Oxford Childrens' Dictionary*, which I discussed on page 86, and a hard-backed copy is supplied with the Spellmaster. When you have a word on the Spellmaster's screen, you can display the number of the page in the dictionary where you'll find that word. This means that if you need to know more about the word, for example, check the meaning, find out whether it's a noun or a verb, or see which endings you can add, you can turn to the correct page very quickly.

If your pupil is uncertain about a letter in a word, he can type a question mark instead of that letter. For example, *leo?ard* will produce *leopard* and *leotard*. If you type *le??ard* you will be offered *leeward* as well. This facility is wonderful if a child gets stuck with a crossword and, of course, can be used for building word lists. I typed in *?ar* and was offered nine words, but you need to be careful, because they were not all suitable for an *ar* list. The words *ear* and *oar* do not belong on the list with words like *car*. Ask your pupil to select the words that will be useful for him to have on his list and reject any that don't have the correct sound.

If you want the Spellmaster to supply more letters in a word, but it doesn't matter how many, you can use the * key. This is very good for prefixes and suffixes, because they are different lengths. When you type *employ**, you will be given several words including *employer* and *employment*.

If your pupil is doing a project and he needs words that are not stored in the Spellmaster, he can add up to 50 extra words in a User List. For example, he may want *carbon-dating*, if he is writing about archaeology. Once the word is entered, it stays in the User List until he deletes it. Be careful to check the spelling before the word is entered.

The Spellmaster has several games which I list below.

Flashcards

This gives reading practice and can increase vocabulary.

Spelling Bee

You see a word, have to look at it carefully then, when the screen is blank, you type it in. This encourages the child to study the letter combinations and separate the word into syllables.

Hangman

This is challenging, but fun. It emphasises the use of vowels, makes you aware of the letters we use most, and also draws attention to the most common letter combinations.

Jumble

This is useful if the pupil's User List is made up of words that he has been asked to learn to spell, because it takes each word and jumbles the letters up. The child has to type in the words correctly.

Wordblaster

My favourite, although I wouldn't use it with young children or those whose reading level is fairly basic. The Spellmaster builds up a word, a letter at a time, and you have to guess the word before it is complete and then type it in correctly. You can choose the word size and the speed, and it will soon become obvious that it is easier to use longer words. Therefore you need a reasonably good vocabulary to succeed in this game.

The Spellmaster will not warn you about words like *there* and *their*, which the book *Spell it yourself* does (see page 88). You will have to look in the accompanying dictionary if you need to check which one to use.

Franklin produce other spellcheckers that are more suitable for students on A-level or university courses. These incorporate a thesaurus, which suggests words with similar meanings. This is a great help if you find yourself using one word too often when writing essays.

You and your pupil will benefit much more from a spellchecker if you use it together. I have seen 'button-mad' children who enjoy the sensation of making words appear and disappear without making any attempt to even look at them, let alone read them. If you use the spellchecker together, you can monitor how well your pupil is doing, ask him questions and point out revision tips. It can be a very valuable, portable learning tool.

Spellcheckers that are part of a word-processor

There are many different word-processors and I happen to use WordPerfect 5.1, which is fairly old. When you use a word-processor, you can do everything that a typewriter does, and much more, such as checking your spelling. You can check just one word, or a whole passage. When the word-processor's spellchecker finds a misspelt word, it highlights that word and gives a list of words that hopefully includes the one you want. It's then up to you to find the correct one. It's surprising how quickly children can *read* the word they want, even though they can't *spell* it. When you recognise the correct word, you need press only one key and the correct word replaces the incorrect one.

In some respects my word-processor's spellchecker is less flexible than the Franklin Spellmaster. You can't use a ? or * to take the place of letters that you are unsure about. Nevertheless, when you are using a computer, a built-in spellchecker is very convenient, and the fact that it searches your entire text and highlights misspellings and also silly typing errors, such as *weel* instead of *well*, is invaluable. It also has a thesaurus.

As I have said earlier, not all spellcheckers are equally good, but I was pleasantly surprised to find that my weird spellings of *giraffe* and **knowledge** (see page 89) posed no problems for the spellchecker on my word-processor.

As with the Spellmaster, my spellchecker gives no help about when to use **there** and **their**. Added to that, there are no games on it, and you can't use it on long car journeys!

Two, to and too

Normally *two*, number 2, doesn't cause any trouble, but I take the opportunity to point out that words connected with 2 use *tw*. We have *twelve*, *twenty*, *twin* and *twice*.

On the other hand, the words *to* and *too* often give trouble. *Too* has two meanings.

1. It means 'as well'
   Can I come too?   Can I come *as well*?
2. It means too much of something
   He was too tall.   (too much height)
   The water was too cold.   (too much coldness)

On all other occasions use *to*. If your mind goes blank and you can't decide which one is right, go for *to*, because that's the one that we use most. One more point, if you listen to what you say, *to* is a very short word, whereas *too* has a definite *oo* sound.

Dictation sentences
Paul is going to play too.   She sang too loudly.
It was too hot to run.   David has two kittens and a dog too.
Dad is going to make a cake and put two candles on it.

There and their

In order to help with the spelling of these words, I point out that they both start with **the**.

their means **belonging to them**

The children can leave *their* bags.   (the bags *belonging to them*)

Gareth and James made *their* go-cart.   (the go-cart *belonging to them*)

I always link **there** with **here** and **where**. 'Where is it? Here or there?' For one thing, the spelling of the three words is similar. Sometimes it helps to make a list of the words that are likely to follow **there**. Here are some examples:

there is	there was	there will be	there has been
there are	there were	there goes	there have been

Dictation sentences

There was no pie left.
The children spent all their pocket money.
The grown-ups would like their tea now.

There goes the last bus.
There was no key.
Tell the girls to put their books there.

Books

Finding suitable books

When your child's reading skills are below average, he needs books that are simple to read, but he doesn't want 'baby books'. He wants books that interest children of his age. For example, a ten year old may only have the reading ability (known as the Reading Age) of an average seven year old, but he will want books that interest ten year olds. It is this gap between reading ability and interest that makes it difficult for these children to choose books from ordinary bookshops. In the first part of the list below, which is mostly made up of sets of books my colleagues and I have used and liked, I have indicated the Reading Age and the Interest Level of the books.

I have found that many parents don't like the idea of going into a library, let alone asking for help there. However if you can, I suggest that you go to your local library, without your child at first, and ask to speak to the children's librarian. She will understand about children whose reading ability is below average, but who need books suitable for their age. I have always found librarians extremely helpful. They usually take you to the section you need and also point out some suitable books. They may have some of the books on my list. Sometimes schools are willing to lend out books, if they are confident that the books will be returned promptly and in good condition.

Children vary a great deal in their backgrounds, personalities and maturity, and this is reflected in the type of book they will enjoy. Don't automatically discard a book because it looks a bit dated. Sometimes I apologise to a pupil for introducing a book that is a bit old fashioned, but often a pupil will say, 'Oh that doesn't matter! I like this book!' This reaction is because he can actually *read* the book that I have suggested, and make sense of it without a great struggle.

It's important to remember that there are different kinds of reading. Some books require a lot of effort and concentration. On the other hand, there are books we read easily and we often race through them for the pleasure of finding out what happens in the story. I think that, when we are teaching, we are often so concerned with raising the standard of our pupil's reading by giving him slightly more challenging (and tiring) books each time, that we neglect to give him the chance to zip through a simple story for sheer enjoyment.

Books for children to read

Series	Publishers	Reading Age (yrs)	Interest Level (yrs)
Read and Colour	Schofield and Sims	5	5–6+
Primary Phonics More Primary Phonics	Educators Publishing Service (Obtainable from Better Books)	5–6	5–6+
Oxford Reading Tree	Oxford University Press	5–9.5	5–7+
Fuzzbuzz	Oxford University Press	5–9.5	8–14
Sunshine	Heinemann	5–10	11–16
Bangers and Mash	Longman	5.5–8	5–10
Rescue Reading	Ginn	5.5–10	8–14
Skyways	Collins Educational	6–10	8–12+
Trend	Ginn	6–10+	12–16
I Can Read Books	Heinemann	6.5–7.5	6–7
Thin King Stories	Longman	6.5–8.5	7–10
Five Minute Thrillers	LDA	7–8	10–16
Trog Books	Nelson	7–8.5	7–11
Winners	Hodder and Stoughton	7.5–8.5	9–12
Happy Families	Penguin	7.5–8.5	7–11
Banana Books	Heinemann	7.5–10+	7–11
Bulls-eye Books	Stanley Thornes	8–10+	14–18+
New Windmill Series	Heinemann	9.5–10+	9–14
Pam and Tom	Heaton Place Publishing	10	14–18+
Headwork	Oxford University Press	11	11–14+

Useful reference books for pupils

Spelling Check-list	E. G. Stirling	Available from the author
Which is Witch?	E. G. Stirling	Available from the author
Spell It Yourself	G. T. Hawker	Oxford University Press
The Illustrated Oxford Dictionary		Oxford University Press
The Oxford Children's Dictionary		Oxford University Press
Punctuation in its Place		Hodder and Stoughton

Further reading for parents and teachers

This book doesn't make sens̶ ȼens̶ sens̶ sȼens̶ sense	Jean Augur	British Dyslexia Association
Understanding Dyslexia	T. R. Miles	Amethyst
Help for the Dyslexic Adolescent	E. G. Stirling	Available from the author
The Bangor Dyslexia Teaching System	Elaine Miles	Whurr
Tackling Dyslexia: The Bangor Way	Ann Cooke	Whurr
Dyslexia: Your Questions Answered		British Dyslexia Association
Opening the Door		British Dyslexia Association
The English Language	David Crystal	Penguin
A Little Edge of Darkness	T. and A. Faludy	Jessica Kingsley
Parents on Dyslexia		Multilingual Matters
Dyslexia: A Parents' Survival Guide	Christine Ostler	Ammonite Books

From time to time, there are programmes on television about helping children to read and spell. Usually there is a companion book published and it's worth popping into your local bookshop to see what's available.

Appendices

Appendix 1 – Intermediate Chart

As I explained in the main part of the book, my Intermediate Chart can be used as a stepping stone, a link, between Chart 1 and Chart 2. You will find three versions of the Intermediate Chart, (Blank, Guide and Keywords) in the Photocopiable Resources section on pages 124–6. There is nothing on this chart that is not on either Chart 1 or Chart 2. The Intermediate Chart overlaps both Chart 1 and Chart 2.

The Intermediate Chart has forty eight letter combinations. Eleven are transferred from Chart 1 and thirty seven are new ones. When you transfer to Chart 2, you will find that you have thirty nine spaces still to fill. So you can see that the Intermediate Chart covers roughly half the work on Chart 2.

The combinations, *ch, sh, th, wh-, -ank, -ink, -unk, -ang, -ing, -ong* and *-ung*, at the bottom of the chart, are the ones that are transferred from Chart 1. These sounds are sometimes still giving trouble. Even if your pupil is quite sure about them, filling in these spaces, after a very quick revision, gives him a flying start with his new chart.

When your pupil has completed the work on the Intermediate Chart, it is easy to transfer the letter combinations onto Chart 2, which will then be half full! I have kept the arrangement of the boxes on the two charts the same as far as possible.

If you decide to use the Intermediate Chart, you can still follow the section about Chart 2, which starts on page 28, and pick out the letter combinations that you need for the Intermediate Chart, leaving the others until later.

Appendix 2 – more 'Look and Say' words

come	give	*here*	*which*
some	have	*there*	*what*
		where	*why*
you	any		*where*
your	many	ever	
they		never	who
their			
	aunt	only	love
mother	uncle		
father	cousin	her	want
sister	nephew		
brother	niece	friend	were

Some of these words, for example *want* and *nephew*, are not really 'Look and Say' words, but they are often needed before they crop up in the lists of regular words. When this happens I introduce them as 'Look and Say' words.

The following remarks about some of the words above may be useful.

give, have	We don't end words with a *v*.
there, their	Both start with *the*.
only	Starts like the word *one ... only one*.
were	We often say, '*We we*re ...'
many	*Man*y a *man* is crazy about football.
who	'Dr Who' may be already known.
friend	The *end* comes at the end. It is the *i* that gives trouble. If you make the i into a matchstick man, he will be your friend in the middle of the word and separate the Blend *fr* from *end*.

friend

You and your pupil will probably think of your own ways of remembering more of these awkward words.

Appendix 3 – days, months etc. and number words

Days	Months		Seasons
Monday	1 January	Jan	Spring
Tuesday	2 February	Feb	Summer
Wednesday	3 March	Mar	Autumn
Thursday	4 April	Apr	Winter
Friday	5 May	May	
Saturday	6 June	Jun	
Sunday	7 July	Jul	**School holidays**
	8 August	Aug	Easter
	9 September	Sep	Summer
	10 October	Oct	Christmas
	11 November	Nov	
	12 December	Dec	

Number words

1 one	11 eleven			1st	first
2 two	12 twelve	20 twenty		2nd	second
3 three	13 thirteen	30 thirty		3rd	third
4 four	14 fourteen	40 forty		4th	fourth
5 five	15 fifteen	50 fifty		5th	fifth
6 six	16 sixteen	60 sixty		6th	sixth
7 seven	17 seventeen	70 seventy		7th	seventh
8 eight	18 eighteen	80 eighty		8th	eighth
9 nine	19 nineteen	90 ninety		9th	ninth
10 ten		100 hundred		10th	tenth
	1,000 thousand	1,000,000 million			

I have deliberately left a gap above the word *twenty* because I wanted to line it up with *two* and *twelve*, to make the point that all these words, which are connected with the number two, start with *tw*. *Twice* and *twins* also have *tw*. You can look across other rows and see similarities and differences in spelling.

Appendix 4 – spelling rules

We don't end words with these letters

There are some letters that generally speaking we don't find at the end of English words. Below is a list of these letters and the endings that take their places, and then a note about each one.

Don't use	Use		Don't use	Use
single *s*	*-se*		*i*	*-y*
single *z*	*-ze*		*j*	*-ge*
v	*-ve*		*u*	*-w*

If we ended words with a single *s*, they would look like plurals. So to prevent the *s* from coming right at the end, we add an *e* which is not necessary for the sound of the word. Here are a few examples.

cheese	horse	nurse	please	because
goose	house	noise	sense	raise

Another way we avoid using a single *s* to end a word, is to use a soft *c*, which makes the *s* sound. All the *ace* and *ice* words do this, and so do words like *dance*, *fence* and *prince*.
    Similarly we don't end words with a single *z*. Once more we add an *e* to complete the word.

freeze	breeze	squeeze	snooze
sneeze	wheeze	maize	booze

The *e* after the *v* in these words acts in exactly the same way, preventing the *v* from being the final letter.

have	active	love	dove
give	expensive	glove	shove
live	attractive	above	

Another point, the words in the third and fourth columns make the sound *uv* in spite of their vowel being *o*.

We do use some words that end in *i*, but they are really foreign words. Examples are *spaghetti* (Italian), *muesli* (German), *rabbi* (Hebrew), *kiwi* (Maori), *tandoori* (Urdu) and *origami* (Japanese). I have found that these words don't normally give trouble, perhaps because they are so unusual. Apart from foreign words, we use *y* instead of an *i* to end words. This has already been shown in various places on Chart 2. Here are a few reminders:

funny	hungry	baby	day	fly
fancy	money	allergy	boy	

Just like an *i*, the *y* can be a long or short vowel. In the first three columns it is short.

We don't use *j* at the end of a word. The *age*, *-dge* and soft *g* lists show that we use *ge* instead, as you can see in *wage*, *bridge* and *college*.

There's a link between *u* and *w*, and we use *w*, not *u*, to end words. If you look at Boxes 12 and 15 on Chart 2, you will see that they each have a vowel that can be followed by *u* or *w*. In each case we use the combination that has the *w* for the end of a word.

sauce	*pause*	*clause*	*loud*	*count*
saw	*paw*	*claw*	*allow*	*cow*

The ending **ed** has three different sounds

When we write about something that happened in the past, we add *ed* to the verb, except in a few irregular cases. This can make the sound *d*, *t* or *ud*. I find with many pupils I have to stress the fact that the ending is *ed* even though it doesn't always sound like it.

d	*t*	*ud*
played	helped	wanted
oiled	walked	hunted

i *before* e *except after* c ... *most of the time!*

Although this well known rule doesn't always work, it is useful for many words where the two letters make the sound *ee*.

chief	field	achieve	believe
thief	shield	priest	belief

brief	piece	siege	mischief
grief	niece	relief	handkerchief

The following group have a *c* and therefore the *e* comes before the *i*.

ceiling	receive	receipt	deceive

So far the rule is working. However in the words below, where the two letters make the sound *ay*, I'm sorry to say the rule doesn't work.

eight	weigh	neighbour	reign
vein	weight	reindeer	freight

Irregular plurals

Most of our plurals end in *s*, but some are different. We even have a few words where the plural is the same as the singular. The words *sheep* and *deer* are like this, and *fish* can stay the same or add *es*. Here are some common irregular plurals.

man	men	child	children	foot	feet
woman	women	mouse	mice	tooth	teeth
				goose	geese

There are twenty six sheep in the small field.
Mr Jones had thirty seven deer in his herd.

Tom caught three fish.
Tom caught three fishes.

Appendix 5 – further work

You may find that you need to teach letter combinations that are not on Chart 2. I apologise for this, but I had to draw the line somewhere, in order to make the chart manageable. However I have listed some extra letter combinations that I think you may need.

-zz

There are a few words that end in -zz. They could be added to the other double endings in Box 1 on Chart 2.

jazz	fizz	buzz

-ey

It is much more common to use -*y* for the $\breve{i}$ sound at the ends of words, as I have shown on page 53, but there are a few words that use -*ey*.

donkey	money	kidney	valley	journey
monkey	honey	jockey	abbey	turkey

-ous and -ious

When we get the *us* sound at the end of a word, it is spelt *-ous*. Sometimes there is an *i* in front of the *-ous* and then we see three vowels together, most unusual in English.

-ous			-ious	
famous	dangerous	tremendous	serious	furious
nervous	enormous	ridiculous	obvious	previous
jealous	poisonous	marvellous	curious	mysterious

-ti-, -ci- and -si-

Generally, these three letter combinations all make the sound *sh* in words of more than one syllable. The only common exceptions are *cushion, fashion, bishop, warship* and *worship*.

-ti-
We have already seen *ti* making a *sh* sound in the letter combination *-tion*. You can see below that it does the same thing in some other endings.

-tial	-tious	-tient	-tience
confidential	cautious	patient	patience
initial	infectious		
essential	ambitious		

-ci-
These two letters also make a *sh* sound in the middle of some words.

-cial	-cian	-cious
special	musician	delicious
social	optician	suspicious
racial	magician	precious
official	electrician	vicious
artificial	politician	
financial	technician	

-si-
This letter combination only seems to be used in front of *on*.

-sion

revision	explosion	decision	admission
television	division	invasion	permission
tension	occasion	pension	diversion
extension	version	mansion	conclusion

-ui- (oo)

This is an awkward group of letters which appears in some common words.

fruit	juice	suit	bruise	cruise

sc

I can never decide whether the *s* is the silent letter or the *c*, but it really doesn't matter, one of them is silent!

scene	scent	science	scissors

-mn

These words have a silent *n*.

hymn	autumn	column	solemn

Extending **wa-** and **wo-**, into **war-** and **wor-**

As before, you have to pretend that the *a* in the first sound is an *o*, so the *ar* is pronounced *or*, giving us the word *war*, which we are so familiar with. In the second group, the *or* is pronounced *ur* and so we get the word *work*.

war (wor)		*wor* (wur)	
war	towards	work	worse
warn	reward	word	worry
warm	wardrobe	worm	world
ward	warship	worth	worship
wart		worst	

Answers

The sounds of the letters are different from their names (page 14)

bee yellow tea – B L O T – blot

Unexpected Sounds and Blends (page 27)

Put the rest of the junk on the top step.

Glenda spilt the milk.

Frank is bringing a wet cloth.

The frog can jump and splash and swim.

Dad will get fish and chips.

When will Tim lend me a quid?

Punctuation exercises (page 84)

Version 1

Bob closed the door quietly. He gave his orders in a few minutes. The men crossed the car park being careful to move secretly. Next morning Bob went to see Joe in the room near the canteen. There was a group of men talking excitedly.

Version 2

Bob closed the door. Quietly he gave his orders. In a few minutes the men crossed the car park being careful to move secretly. Next morning Bob went to see Joe. In the room near the canteen there was a group of men talking excitedly.

Punctuated story (page 84)

Again there are parts of this passage that can be punctuated in different ways. For example, did they take chocolate and biscuits, in which case there would be a comma between the two words? The way I have punctuated it, they took chocolate biscuits. To take another example, the phrase, 'to add to their trouble', could follow straight on after the word 'broken', and then the word 'it' would start the next sentence. This would still make sense. I hope that you can see that punctuation really does affect the meaning of the words.

On a hot Monday in June, Rose, Mark and Miles drove up to the Tees on Cross Fell for a picnic they had been planning for some time. They took cans of Coca-Cola, chocolate biscuits, an orange cake, sandwiches and three apples.

'Is it far?' asked Mark, who didn't know that part of England.

'Good heavens no!' laughed Miles. 'We'll be there very soon.'

In ten minutes they had parked the car, unloaded their things, and were enjoying their lunch among the buttercups. They saw lots of white butterflies, and two wasps came to sample the jam in the cake. When they had finished eating, they walked by the river. All of a sudden, Rose yelled. She had slipped and twisted her ankle. Miles looked at Mark.

'What shall we do? She'll never manage to walk back now.'

'We'll have to help her', replied Mark, 'one on each side to give her support.'

The strap on Rose's shoe had broken. To add to their trouble, it had started to rain and they were all soaked when they reached the car.

'We're not having a very good time are we?' moaned Rose, but the others said cheerily they'd had a good time until her accident.

She thought, 'It's all very well for you two!'

'We'll soon be home', continued Miles, 'and when your ankle is attended to, and we've all changed into dry clothes, we can put up our feet and watch the telly.'

For the rest of the journey home, Rose was very quiet. She wished she'd worn more sensible shoes.

Photocopiable resources

CHART 1 COMPLETE

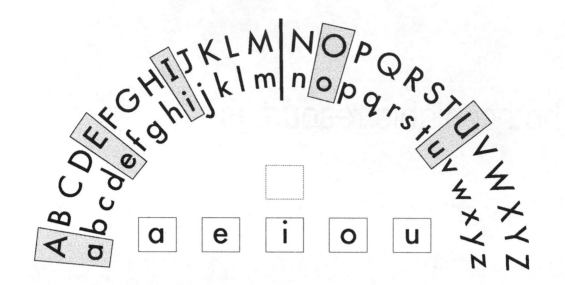

a	e	i	o	u

UNEXPECTED SOUNDS

ch	sh	th	wh-	qu-	-ng	-nk

BLENDS

bl	br	cl	cr	dr	fl	fr
gl	gr	pl	pr	sc	sk	sl
sm	sn	sp	st	sw	tr	tw

-ct	-ft	-lk	-lt	-mp
	-nd	-nt	-sp	-st	

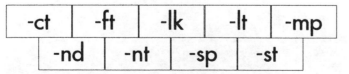

scr	shr	spl	spr
	squ	str	thr	

CHART 1 BLANK

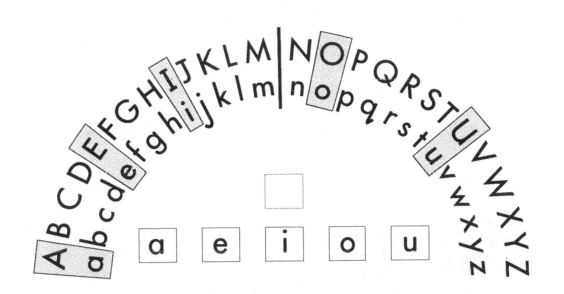

a e i o u

UNEXPECTED SOUNDS

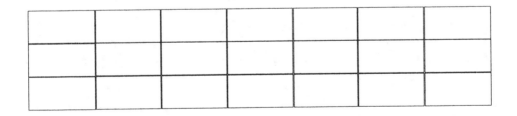

BLENDS

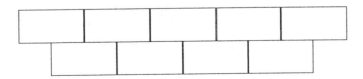

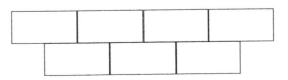

109

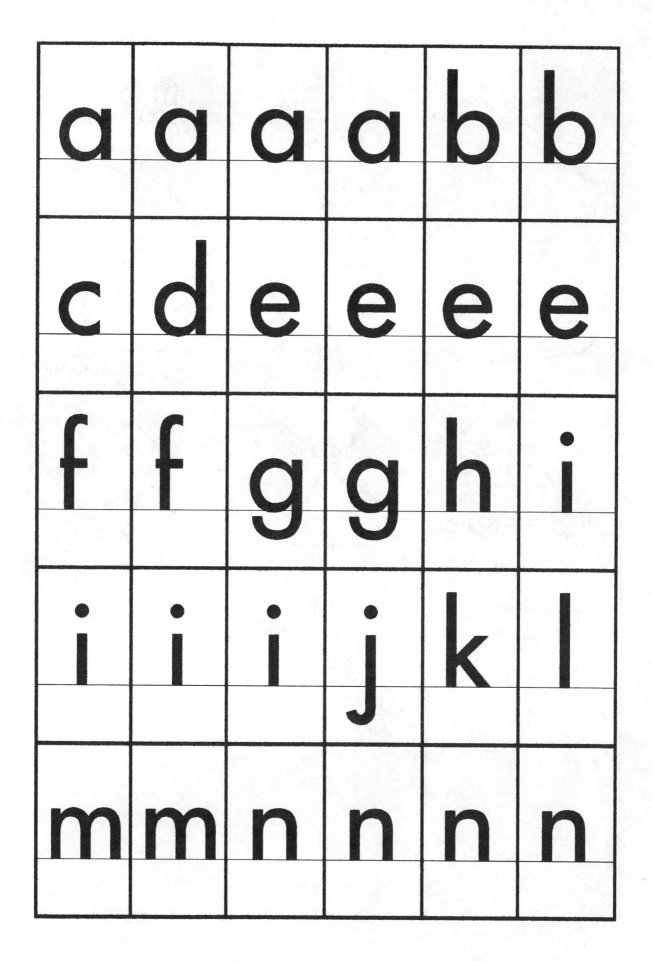

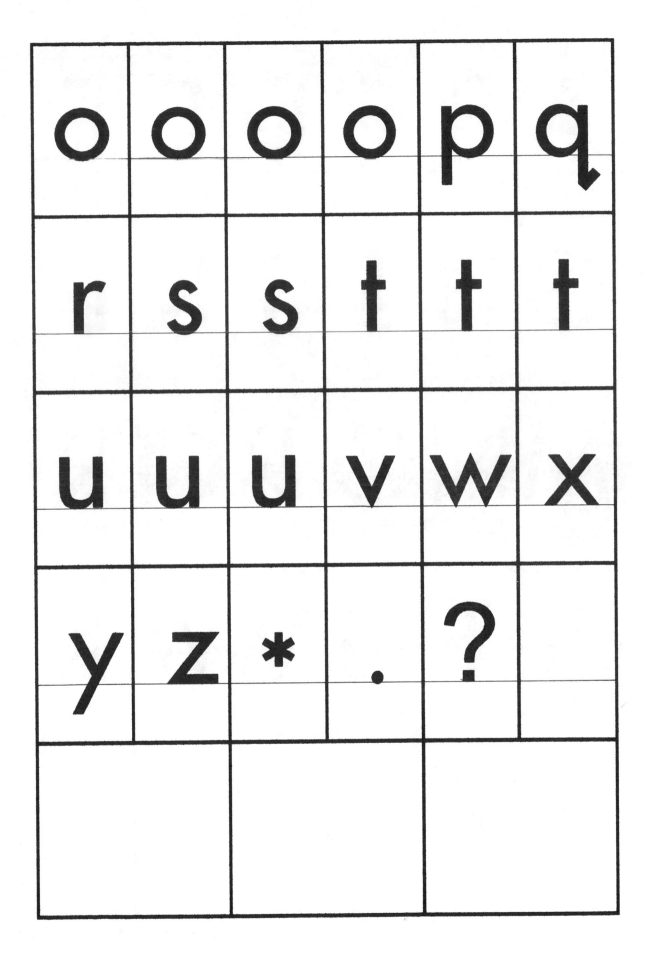

o	o	o	o	p	q
r	s	s	t	t	t
u	u	u	v	w	x
y	z	*	.	?	

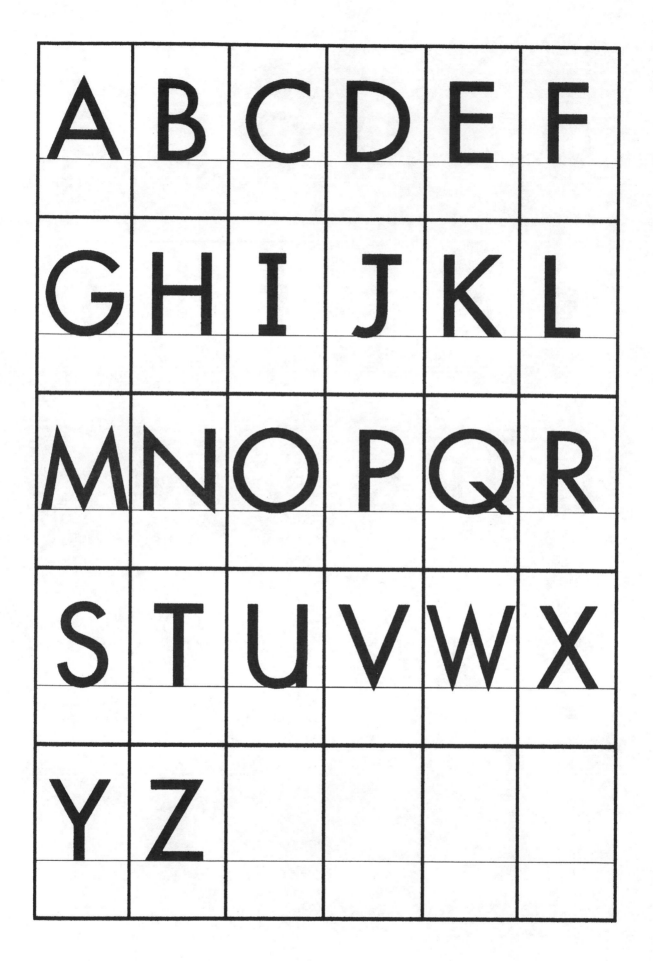

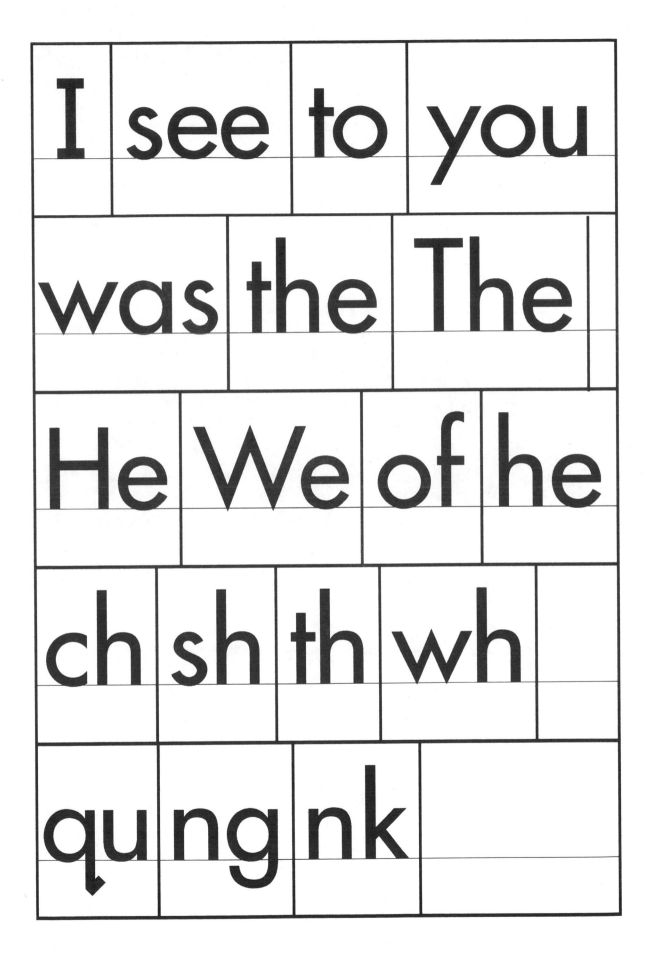

I see to you

was the The

He We of he

ch sh th wh

qu ng nk

CHART 2 BLANK

CHART 2 GUIDE

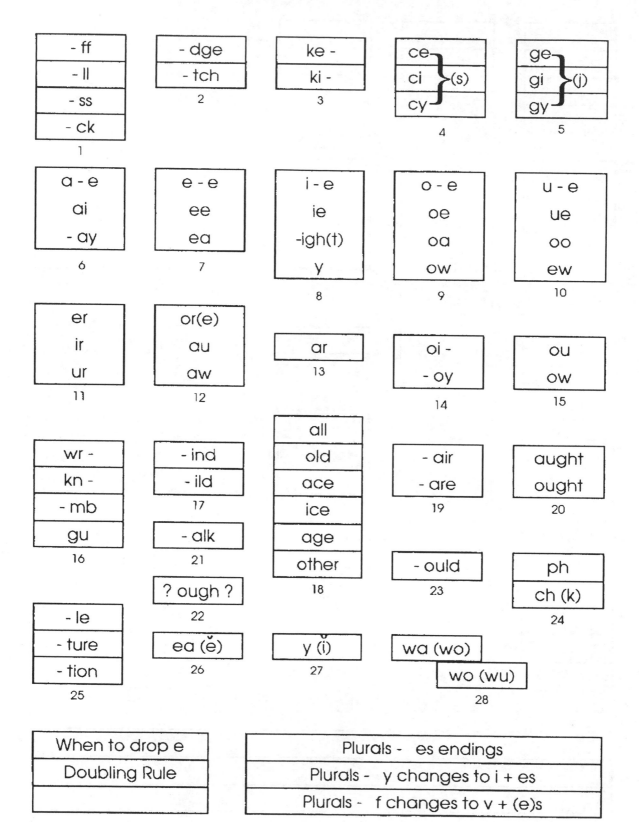

- ff - ll - ss - ck 1	- dge - tch 2	ke - ki - 3	ce ci }(s) cy 4	ge gi }(j) gy 5

a - e
ai
- ay
6

e - e
ee
ea
7

i - e
ie
-igh(t)
y
8

o - e
oe
oa
ow
9

u - e
ue
oo
ew
10

er
ir
ur
11

or(e)
au
aw
12

ar
13

oi -
- oy
14

ou
ow
15

wr -
kn -
- mb
gu
16

- ind
- ild
17

- alk
21

? ough ?
22

all
old
ace
ice
age
other
18

- air
- are
19

- ould
23

aught
ought
20

ph
ch (k)
24

- le
- ture
- tion
25

ea (ĕ)
26

y (ĭ)
27

wa (wo)
wo (wu)
28

When to drop e
Doubling Rule

Plurals - es endings
Plurals - y changes to i + es
Plurals - f changes to v + (e)s

CHART 2 KEYWORDS

cliff	hedge	keep	central	germ
shell	match	kill	city	giant
miss			cycle	gym
sock				

game	Pete	time	home	tune
rain	tree	pie	toe	blue
day	eat	fight	boat	moon
		sky	slow	new

her	pork	car	oil	out
girl	Paul		boy	owl
burn	law			

		ball		
wrong	kind	gold	chair	taught
knife	child	face	spare	bought
lamb		mice		
guess	talk	page		
		mother	could	phone
	? ? ? ? ?			chemist

little				
picture	head	funny	wash	
station			wolf	

take + ing = taking	boxes dishes beaches glasses
fit + ed = fitted	baby - babies fly - flies
	knife - knives leaf - leaves

CHECKLIST OF LETTER COMBINATIONS IN
THE SUGGESTED ORDER OF TEACHING

Name..

	Page	✓		Page	✓		Page	✓
a - e			or(e)			ke		
i - e			er			ki		
o - e			- alk			ou		
u - e			oi -			ow (cow)		
e - e			- oy			wr -		
-ff			ea			- air		
-ll			ȳ			- are		
-ss			y̆			- mb		
-ck			kn-			- tion		
all			ow (snow)			au		
old			oa			aw		
ace			- igh(t)			ph		
ice			ir			ch (k)		
age			ew			- ind		
other			ce			- ild		
ee			ci			ea (ĕ)		
ie			cy			gu		
oe			ge			- ture		
ue			gi			aught		
ar			gy			ought		
oo			- le			?ough?		
- ould			-dge			wa		
ai			-tch			wo		
- ay			ur					

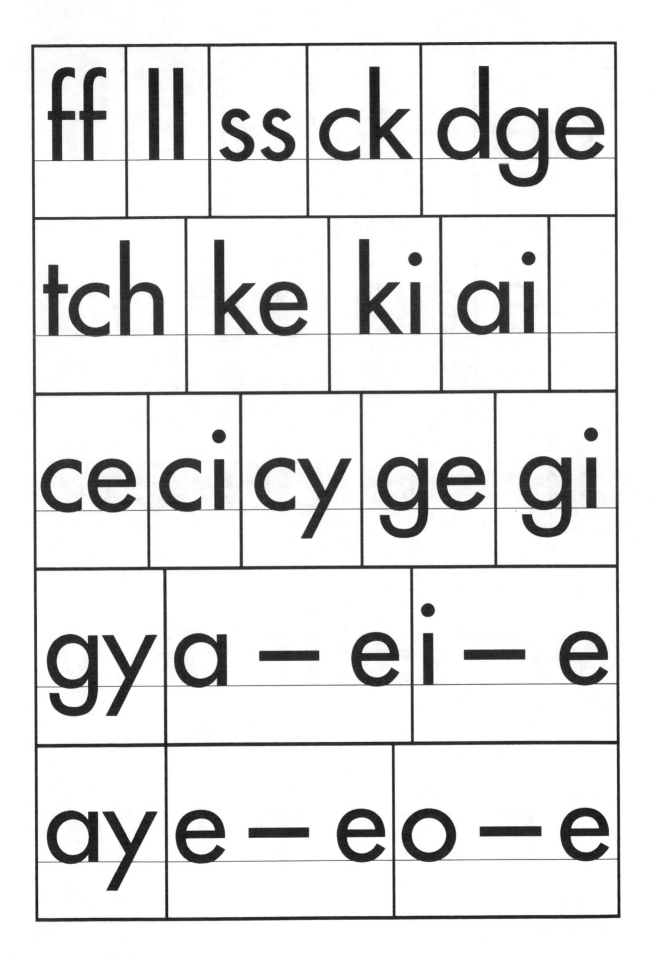

ff | ll | ss | ck | dge

tch | ke | ki | ai

ce | ci | cy | ge | gi

gy | a – e | i – e

ay | e – e | o – e

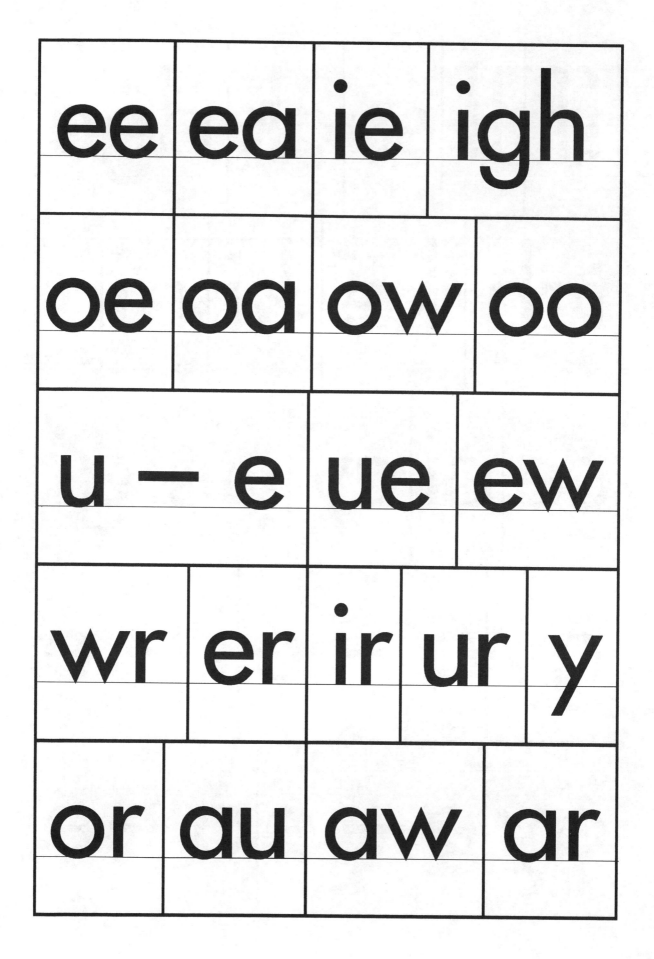

ee ea ie igh

oe oa ow oo

u – e ue ew

wr er ir ur y

or au aw ar

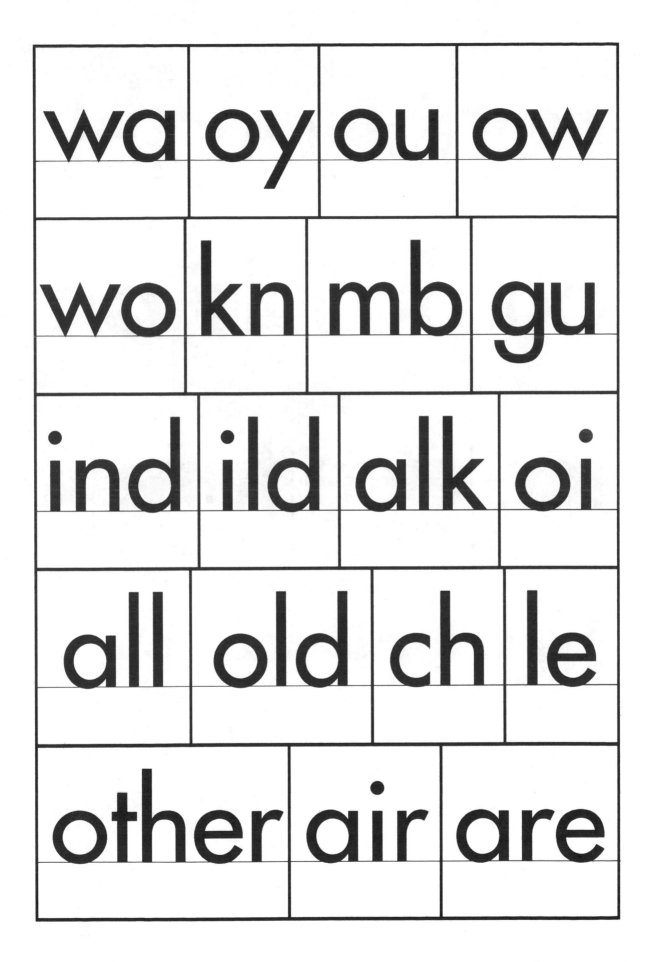

wa	oy	ou	ow
wo	kn	mb	gu
ind	ild	alk	oi
all	old	ch	le
other	air	are	

121

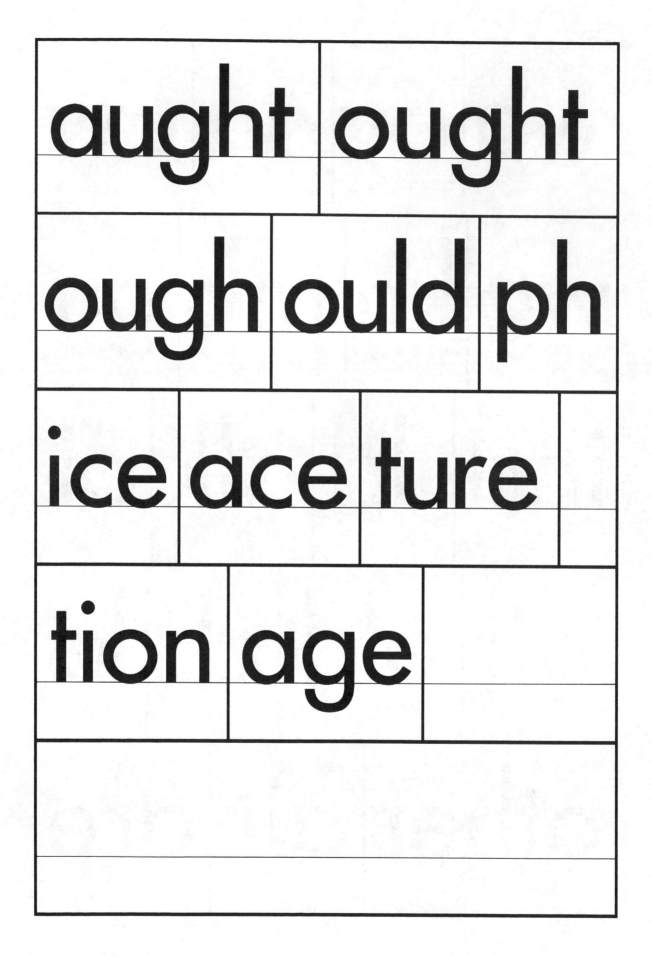

aught	ought
ough	ould	ph
ice	ace	ture
tion	age	

CHART 2 GUIDE

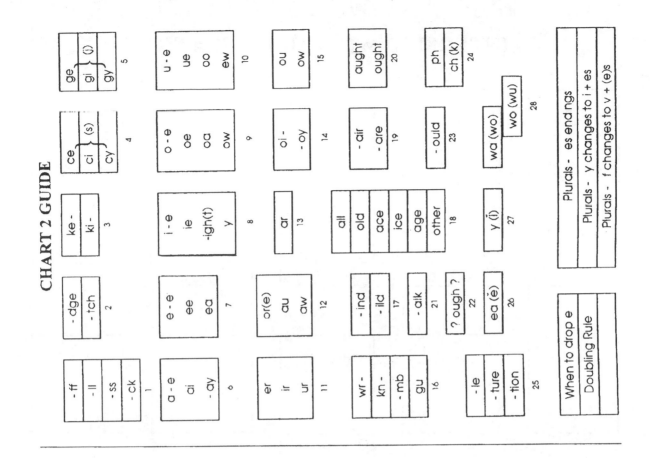

ge	
gi	(j)
gy	
5

ce	
ci	(s)
cy	
4

| ke - |
| ki - |
3

| - dge |
| - tch |
2

| - ff |
| - ll |
| - ss |
| - ck |
1

| u - e |
| ue |
| oo |
| ew |
10

| o - e |
| oe |
| oa |
| ow |
9

| i - e |
| ie |
| -igh(t) |
| y |
8

| e - e |
| ee |
| ea |
7

| a - e |
| ai |
| - ay |
6

| ou |
| ow |
15

| oi - |
| - oy |
14

| ar |
13

| or(e) |
| au |
| aw |
12

| er |
| ir |
| ur |
11

| aught |
| ought |
20

| - air |
| - are |
19

| all |
| old |
| ace |
| ice |
| age |
| other |
18

| - ind |
| - ild |
17

| wr - |
| kn - |
| - mb |
| gu |
16

| ph |
| ch (k) |
24

| - ould |
23

| ? ough ? |
22

| - alk |
21

| wa (wo) |
| wo (wu) |
28

| y (i) |
27

| ea (ĕ) |
26

| - le |
| - ture |
| - tion |
25

| Plurals - es end ngs |
| Plurals - y changes to i + es |
| Plurals - f changes to v + (e)s |

| When to drop e |
| Doubling Rule |

CHART 1 COMPLETE

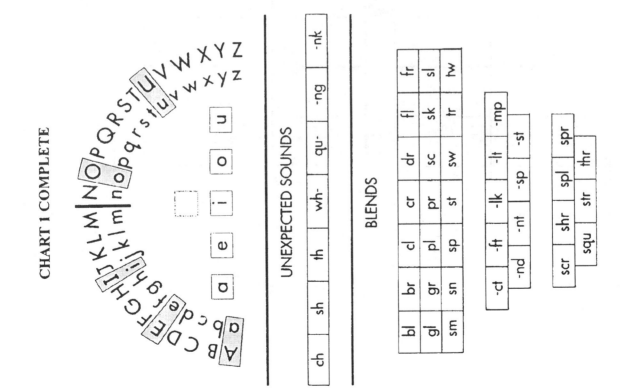

A B C D E F G H I J K L M N O P Q R S T U V W X Y Z
a b c d e f g h i j k l m n o p q r s t u v w x y z

| a | e | i | o | u |

UNEXPECTED SOUNDS

| ch | sh | th | wh- | qu- | -ng | -nk |

BLENDS

bl	br	cl	cr	dr	fl	fr
gl	gr	pl	pr	sc	sk	sl
sm	sn	sp	st	sw	tr	tw

| -ct | -ft | -lk | -lt | -mp |
| -nd | -nt | -sp | -st |

| scr | shr | spl | spr |
| squ | str | thr |

© Walton 123

INTERMEDIATE CHART BLANK

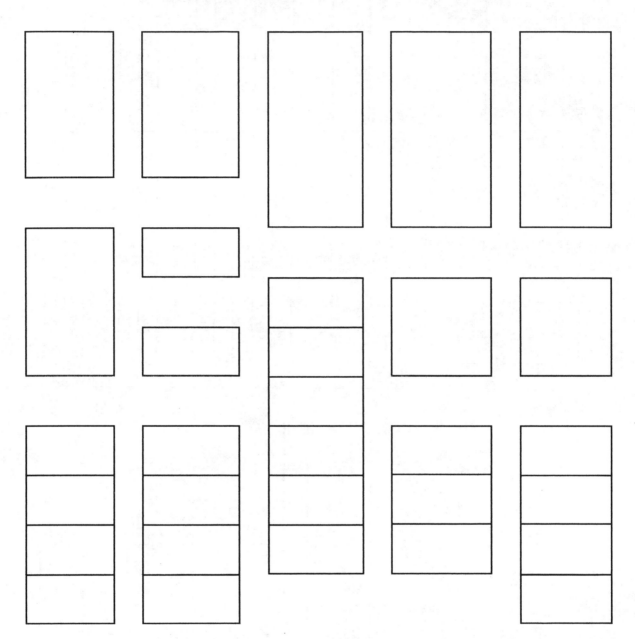

© Walton

INTERMEDIATE CHART GUIDE

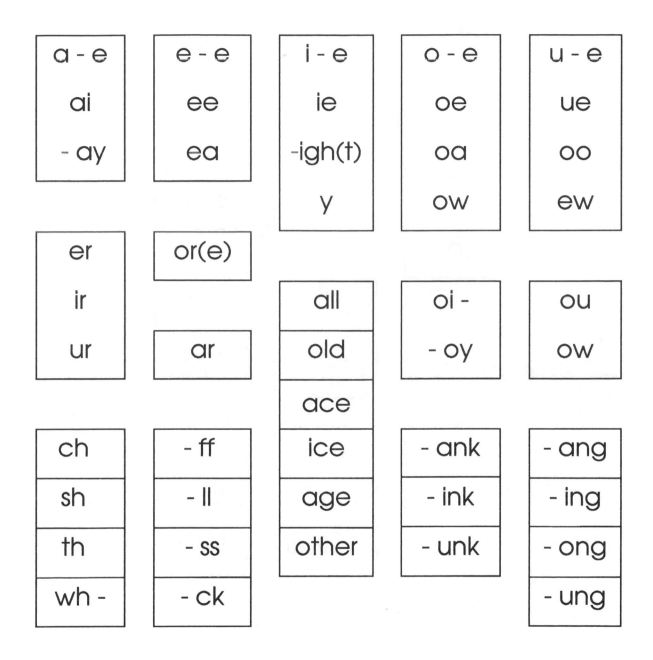

a - e	e - e	i - e	o - e	u - e
ai	ee	ie	oe	ue
- ay	ea	-igh(t)	oa	oo
		y	ow	ew

er	or(e)
ir	
ur	ar

all	oi -	ou
old	- oy	ow
ace		
ice		
age		
other		

ch	- ff	- ank	- ang
sh	- ll	- ink	- ing
th	- ss	- unk	- ong
wh -	- ck		- ung

INTERMEDIATE CHART KEYWORDS

game	Pete	time	home	tune
rain	tree	pie	toe	blue
day	eat	fight	boat	moon
		sky	slow	new

her	pork
girl	
burn	car

ball	oil	out
gold	boy	owl
face		

chip	cliff	mice	bank	bang
shop	shell	page	pink	king
thin	miss	mother	junk	song
when	sock			lung

Addresses

Dyslexia Unit
University of Wales, Bangor
Bangor
Gwynedd
LL57 2DG

British Dyslexia Association
98 London Road
Reading
Berkshire
RG1 5AU

Better Books Ltd
3 Paganel Drive
Dudley
West Midlands
DY1 4AZ

Ammonite Books
58 Coopers Rise
Godalming
Surrey
GU7 2NJ

Franklin UK
11–12 Windmill Business Village
Brooklands Close
Sunbury on Thames
Middlesex
TW16 7DY

Heaton Place Publishing
Heaton Place
169 Midland Road
Royston
Barnsley
S71 4BZ

E. G. Stirling
114 Westbourne Road
Sheffield
S10 2QT

Taskmaster Ltd
Morris Road
Leicester
LE2 6BR

Index

MATHS WORDS by MARGARET WALTON

ISBN 0 9526508 0 0

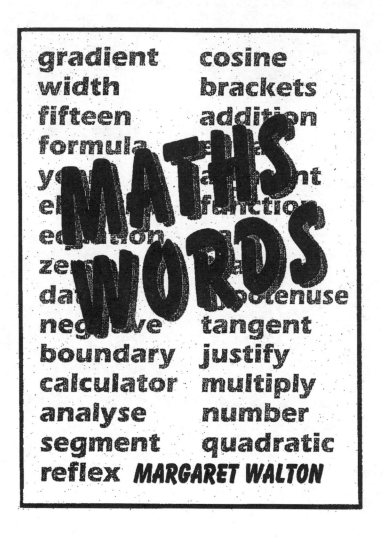

This booklet was written as a direct response to the needs of a 14 year-old dyslexic boy who scored very badly in his maths exams, largely because he couldn't read many of the key words, not because he couldn't do the maths. "Maths Words" is an alphabetical checklist of over 600 words that may appear in GCSE maths examinations. It is primarily intended to give reading practice and does not include definitions.

A6   48 pages   Available from Taskmaster